Feng Shui Made Easy

FENG SHUI
MADE EASY

Designing Your Life with the
Ancient Art of Placement

Updated and Revised Edition, 2010

WILLIAM SPEAR

North Atlantic Books
Berkeley, California

Published by
North Atlantic Books
P.O. Box 12327
Berkeley, California 94712

Illustrations © by Sharon Rothman
Book design by Brad Greene

Printed in the United States of America

Grateful acknowledgment is given for permission to print excerpts from the following works:

Shambhala: The Sacred Path of the Warrior, by Chogyam Trungpa, 1988; reprinted by arrangement with Shambhala Publications, Inc., 300 Massachusetts Avenue, Boston, MA, 02115.

The Bates Method for Better Eyesight Without Glasses, by W. H. Bates, M. D., © 1920, reprinted by permission of Henry Holt and Company, Inc., New York.

Conversations with Isaiah Berlin, © Copyright Éditions du Félin, 1992. First published in English by Peter Halban Publishers, London, and Scribner & Sons, New York.

Feng Shui Made Easy: Designing Your Life with the Ancient Art of Placement is sponsored by the Society for the Study of Native Arts and Sciences, a nonprofit educational corporation whose goals are to develop an educational and cross-cultural perspective linking various scientific, social, and artistic fields; to nurture a holistic view of arts, sciences, humanities, and healing; and to publish and distribute literature on the relationship of mind, body, and nature.

North Atlantic Books' publications are available through most bookstores. For further information, visit our website at www.northatlanticbooks.com or call 800-733-3000.

Library of Congress Cataloging-in-Publication Data
Spear, William.
    Feng Shui made easy : designing your life with the ancient art of placement / William Spear. — Updated and rev. ed.
        p. cm.
    Includes bibliographical references and index.
    ISBN 978-1-55643-938-4
    1. Feng shui. 2. Yi jing. I. Title.
    BF1779.F4S65 2010
    133.3'337—dc22
                                                                2010022428

        2 3 4 5 6 7 8 9 UNITED 16 15 14 13 12 11

The new edition of this book is lovingly dedicated
to the memory of my Mother, with profound appreciation
for her example of selfless giving; and
to my wife Joan, with love and gratitude; and
to the millions of men and women who inspire all of us
through their passionate efforts to care for Mother Earth,
with my heartfelt gratitude.

Contents

Acknowledgments

It is an honor to express here my deep appreciation and heartfelt thanks to the many people who have made this book possible. Gathering material for the first edition of this book began long before I realized that I would write it—preceding my focus on *feng shui* and the extraordinary body of knowledge that surrounds it. Like many young boys, I did not realize as a child how greatly my father's fascination with one particular subject would influence me later in life; now, as a grown man with sons of my own, I can still see the sparkle in his eyes when we worked on magic squares together. It has had a lasting influence. The first edition, therefore, was dedicated to him.

Years after my father passed away, I was deeply grateful to become even closer to my mother, a blessing that reminded me of her presence behind the scenes when puzzles and games littered the living room floor of my childhood. Up to her final moments with us, she remained a living example of generosity to those in need, as "giving" was always her raison d'être. It is with endless gratitude for my life that I therefore dedicate this revised and updated edition to her memory.

Joan, my wife and partner now into our fourth decade together, deserves more credit than I usually reveal. Her efforts behind the scenes while I traveled, taught, counseled, and contemplated my navel supported me without interruption. That she is the mother of our three children is a bonus beyond compare; to experience her prolific creative force in my life remains my most fortunate blessing.

Even now, I cannot fail to acknowledge Michio Kushi and his late wife, Aveline, who together were both teachers and friends whose life and work influenced me greatly. Their tireless efforts on behalf of so many people are of immeasurable value. I offer my warmest thanks to both of them. Takashi Yoshikawa, the undisputed master of Nine Star Ki, helped me to deepen my understanding in many ways and continued to be an invaluable source of wisdom until his passing in 2006. Sharon Rothman happily sketched many more illustrations than appear herein and rose to the occasion of the new edition with great enthusiasm. Hisae Matsuda at North Atlantic Books has been a cheerful contact from afar, always there to move my work forward and improve the final product; John Vias, a masterful copy editor, helped to make the manuscript more readable; Brad Greene added his considerable design talents with special attention to many details. I am grateful to all three of them for their support. The complete eleventh-hour editing by Whitney Turk will, I hope, lead to more collaborations in the future. Despite a very busy schedule and other pressing demands, it did not go unnoticed that she came with determination, focus, and skill to the job. I am most appreciative for her input. Luisa de Castro, my personal assistant, has worked consistently as an extraordinary professional, office manager, errand runner, and all-around friend since the early days following the publication of the first edition. Much of my success is as a result of her tireless efforts on my behalf. Having Luisa in my life is one of my most fortunate blessings. Of course, clients and students to this day continue to challenge my every word, constantly calling me to task in their search for clarity. Each of them has given me far more than they may realize. I thank them all for their feedback and valuable comments. My sister, Patricia Lemer, made invaluable suggestions on the section about children's environments in the new edition, as well as helping me make numerous improvements throughout the original work; her support was always available, for which I feel very blessed. It was she who suggested I contact Richard Grossinger, the publisher at North Atlantic Books, whose initial communication with me was both welcoming and open-hearted—and has remained so. A special friendship with him and his wife, Lindy, has grown into a most pleasant bonus.

The reader should be absolutely clear that the contributions of those I have mentioned, and the few I may have inadvertently omitted, were related only to style, context, and order. Any inaccuracies, lack of clarity, or oversights are mine alone.

Finally, to my amazing sons, I offer my endless love and thanks. Jonah, Joshua, and Micah watched me come and go at all hours of the day and night, while working, traveling, and writing the first edition; now I watch them soar into their worlds as their own trajectories become more focused and powerful. I am so proud of each of them that I frequently have to temper my bragging in the presence of new friends. I am so pleased to be known as their father instead of having burdened them with being "his son." They possess vast universes of wisdom, maturity, and personal power as a result of the choices they've made since the first edition was released in November 1995. Watching them apply what they've learned so effortlessly growing up reinforces my belief that this is all just a natural way of being.

And to my wife, Joan, I declare my everlasting love, for all that she has given and continues to provide through her endless support, constant encouragement, and lifelong commitment. It will be Joan who writes the next big book that matters, beginning where I have ended. She is far wiser and more courageous now, her relationship with the earth more profound and inspiring than I could have ever imagined. And she is even more beautiful than when we met thirty-five years ago.

William Spear, Litchfield, Connecticut
Autumn 2010

Preface to the 2010 Edition

The world seems a very different place since the first edition of this book was released in 1995, and so it was important for me to take a new look at this thing called "feng shui." While most of my perspectives on the essence of this body of knowledge have not changed significantly, it has become more apparent that our environments—both inner and outer—are of great concern to all of us interested in a better world. Two words that define the decade we have just lived through are "consciousness" and "ecology." So it is with reverence and gratitude that I have the opportunity to contribute this updated and revised edition of *Feng Shui Made Easy.*

On the evening of the original work's release, I had the occasion to speak at Alternatives, a popular speakers' venue at St. James Church, Piccadilly, in London. The anticipation and excitement in the capacity audience of 450 enthusiastic guests was palpable when I arrived that night, as I had already achieved minor celebrity status in the U.K. Thanks to the advance press and a few highly visible interviews, feng shui was everywhere, and as the architectural editor of London's *Sunday Times* told his readers, I was "*the* feng shui man"—not a bad preface to meeting my public. I had already founded the International Feng Shui Society and lectured extensively to thousands of people throughout the U.K. and Europe, so the evening lecture seemed like an ideal chance to push the boundaries even further. The book was behind me now—not in front—and I wanted to deliver a memorable talk that night, offering something other than what I'd written. Those words filled the dozens of new books in cartons behind me. It would soon surprise everyone that the book's first printing would sell out in ten days. Feng shui had truly arrived in the West.

The talk I gave that evening began with reflections about the nature of consciousness, the ways in which we think and develop and how we see the world differently according to our individual perspectives. I went on to suggest that our greatest concern must eventually be our inner and outer environments, the world of our own consciousness and the natural world we inhabit. As such, I introduced the idea of how we as a species had mistakenly acted in ways that ignored our responsibility to protect the ecological treasures around us, and in particular, that our own collective behavior was slowly wreaking havoc on the world's oceans. Toxic contamination of the seas was an issue, I suggested, as were overfishing and the destruction of coral reefs and marshlands. But my biggest concern was the damage done to marine mammals by low-frequency sonar used for testing and defense. Dolphins and whales, mammals with extraordinary intelligence, were dying because of the cacophony of sound we were blasting beneath the deep blue sea. This primordial assault on the senses was also reflected above the surface of the water; the world was becoming too loud for anyone to think clearly. We need silence and a return to nature now more than ever, I said.

It soon became clear that only a small number of those present in the audience were aware of these issues, and fewer still wanted me to continue my talk on this track. Instead, people from the audience became restless and disturbed, as some actually blurted out questions about "the wealth corner" or "tell us some secrets" and made it quite clear that they'd come there expecting something very different from what they were hearing. At one point, I stopped to defend myself, saying, "You can read all those things in the book. I want to take this time to talk about feng shui and the planet." It wasn't long before some people actually stood up and left, while those who seemed to appreciate the direction that my talk was going urged those who objected to quiet down and listen. I introduced the idea of "a day of silence on the oceans on 09/09/99" as an opportunity to stop, look, and listen to what we were collectively allowing to happen to our most precious resource.

As I concluded my talk, the response was as polarized as one could imagine. Frustrated and disappointed, many stormed out, grumbling that it was "a waste of time" and "he didn't talk about feng shui at all." Others crowded the front, eager to shake my hand and congratulate me on the book and the talk. The half who couldn't leave fast enough balanced the half that gave me a standing ovation. The organizers later told me they'd never before had such a strong response to a talk—both positive and negative—with demands for refunds balanced by requests to have me speak again as soon as possible. I remember clearly how so much passion was expressed in the room that night, all in such a short period of time.

The world is not any smaller than it was then, but it is clear to me that we are much closer together now. Technology, for better or worse, has made it possible for us to be aware of events that occur across a distant horizon, in faraway lands, where wars in deserts and mountain ranges make the evening news, where starvation and genocide are given the same sound bites as greed and unstoppable consumerism. We are now able to see vertically as well, up into the reaches of outer space and other worlds and down into the depths of the oceans' deepest trenches. Hiding the results of our behavior and our unconscious, arrogant way of life is no longer possible; moreover, correcting this reckless course may not be an easy thing to do. The lines of demarcation between all things—inner and outer, animals with legs and those with fins, or believers and nonbelievers—are slowly disappearing. Our interdependency with all living beings on this small green island has come front and center. We are all in this together.

If I thought feng shui were only a matter of hanging crystals and painting walls, I would have moved on to something more enduring, less conditional and superficial, long ago. By the turn of this century, the media was awash with feature stories on feng shui candles, feng shui haircuts, and computer applications that could be downloaded in an instant. Society had mercilessly bastardized feng shui and reduced it to a senseless common denominator. Like so many other things, feng shui was sadly degraded as minimally trained consultants sprang up overnight ready to lead the way. I recall one young feng shui consultant from the West Coast who wanted to take an intermediate course with me who, after two weekends of study, had gotten her certificate from one of the more visible feng shui "schools." I had established certain criteria for prospective participants in this intermediate workshop so as to be certain to have a more experienced group. She insisted that she was well trained but asked quite innocently, "What's the *I Ching*?" Ironically, as the ground on which feng shui was built, the study of the Book of Changes must be the start of every authentic consultant's education—not interior design, astrology, or furniture placement. We need to know more about consciousness in order to be clear, not just players full of tricks and secrets. Feng shui will always be more about being than doing.

In the years since the first edition was released, my focus has remained more on the inner world and the extraordinary study of the nature of consciousness. It has been my privilege to be of service in many areas where natural disasters have decimated villages and populations, where nothing was left "outside" to use the "art of placement." That we are all one is inescapable; however, communicating this reality remains my biggest challenge. With that in mind, I choose here to revise and re-release *Feng Shui Made Easy* with three new, helpful chapters that add to our attention beyond the arrangement of things—a recovery of our unique relationship with children, health, and nature. My three sons are now grown men, capable and vibrant. I'd like to think that the environment in which they were raised had something to do with that, so I offer first a new section on feng shui for children's environments. Maybe I'll have a chance to try out these teachings when grandchildren appear!

As a macrobiotic teacher for nearly forty years, health has been foremost in my study and practice. Walking into people's homes where money or marriage issues were the reason for the consultation, I couldn't help but notice that both the food in the pantry and my client's health overshadowed all other matters. It seemed fruitless to tell them where to put the bed if dinner was going to be yet another takeout from the local fast food restaurant. No number of the finest crystals hung anywhere can have as much of a lasting impact as a shift in consciousness to improve one's diet and way of life. Thus, I include a new chapter on feng shui and health.

Finally, and by no means last in importance, feng shui and ecology broadens the importance of this timeless practice to rediscover how the ancients viewed our relationship with nature. One need not look too far to consider how important this topic is now and to the future of our species. There is no longer any time to waste; indeed, we are on the cusp of major changes in the environment that demand we change our ways as fast as we are able. Together with the chapter on health, this new addition is one I hope will make an important difference in your world.

I am humbled again by the task of writing a book—as even rewriting and revising this one has been a major effort. Mistakes that remain are my own, though I owe an immense debt of gratitude to so many who have supported this project from its inception to this, the finished, imperfect product. May all who read this book benefit in some way from its teachings. It is you, the reader, my student and my teacher, to whom I bow in humility as we walk together in health and peace.

Litchfield, Connecticut
Autumn 2010

Introduction to the 1995 First Edition

During World War II, my father was a cryptanalyst who never left Washington, DC, where he and his army pals labored over coded messages intercepted from the enemy. UNIVAC computers as big as a house were still no match for the human brain. He adored puzzles, games of Twenty Questions, crosswords, codes of any kind, and challenging mathematical problems.

Before I could count past ten, Dad showed me a way numbers could move in a special pattern. Sitting down with paper and pencil, he taught me how to construct a magic square. Tic tac toe got old fast, but with the "secret pattern," I could create magic squares all day. Every number in every square had to be placed following the pattern of movement we learned from Dad. He taught my sister and me the spatial arrangement of the whole—how each part related to all the others. When we filled in the magic square, the pattern began to emerge—columns and rows were in relationship; beginnings and endings were not accidental. Everything fit because of the rules. We could tell at a glance if something was off. When I was given coded messages, I had to consider the rules of probability. Common words like "I "or "the" were starting points, and a good understanding of sentence structure made breaking the codes much easier. We began passing notes in code; I was expected to respond using the code, which at first was not hard to break. I had probability, integration, and visualization spoon-fed to me before I stepped into kindergarten.

By playing with secret codes, we learned the statistical frequency of vowels and consonants in sentences, double-letter possibilities, sequences of words, and a myriad of other code-breaking tricks. A magical world—open only to those who knew the secret code—was beginning to form. My sister and I would sit for hours assembling jigsaw puzzles on the coffee table. An early puzzle might be fifty pieces depicting a golden puppy on a pale green pillow; soon, there were 250- and 500-piece puzzles of flower gardens and jars of jelly-beans—considerably more challenging! When we'd master these, before a new one was purchased, we'd turn all the pieces over and do it in green or gray using only shapes as our guide. We solved simple crosswords handily in our spare time; we handled cryp-tograms and mazes from children's magazines with ease. Soon, we tackled the more complex offerings from the local newspapers or the back pages of Sunday magazines. And our magic squares grew rapidly, soon covering hundreds of numbers at a time. We knew the pattern, the way, and the secret. No doubt Dad couldn't predict the connection I would make years later.

At summer camp when I was fifteen, I came across a copy of the strangest book I'd ever seen. One of my camp counselors was read-ing—or more like talking to—a Chinese book of fortune telling called the *I Ching*. Part of each chapter made absolutely no sense: things about farmers on their way to the market, the wagon wheel break-ing, the sun beginning to rot the fruit, and so on. But the explana-tions that followed these parts were very intriguing. "Sometimes, when we start to do something we really want, we run into diffi-culty at the beginning...our commitment is challenged, and we can lose it all...perseverance furthers...." Almost every chance I could—especially at night—I'd read a few lines from some chapter while the other kids in my cabin read comic books or had pillow fights. Some days, I'd even sneak away from a soccer game and return to the cabin to pull out my counselor's worn copy of the *I Ching* and read some more. And then one day lightning struck. I turned to the intro-duction and saw it: the diagram of the philosophical foundation on which this oracle was based. This, it said, was the pattern of life itself and the origin of the Book of Change. It was the magic square!

4	9	2
3	5	7
8	1	6

Nine numbers, arranged on the tic tac toe board I'd spent hours expanding, promised to contain the whole universe! It was a way of thinking and seeing so complete, so simple and harmonious, that a quarter of the world's population had used it to develop an entire cosmology containing a unified theory of medicine, religion, economics, science, and art lasting thousands of years. This was the ultimate book of magic. Soon, I got my own copy of the *I Ching* and learned how to use it. "Where one leg is short, the other is long," said the oracle, so it was not long before I began to see the two worlds of spirit and matter. I understood from this obscure passage that the materialism so highly developed in the West was balanced by great poverty and economic hardship in the East. Moreover, the presence of so many religious teachings and systems so highly developed in the East was balanced by societies in the West that in many places were bereft of the deeper appreciation of the invisible world.

Nothing had a greater impact on Chinese-American cultural exchange than the visit of an American president, Richard Nixon, to the People's Republic of China in 1972. Interest in Asian culture in the West blossomed. James Reston, a Pulitzer Prize–winning journalist, received acupuncture for postoperative pain following the emergency removal of his appendix while in China. He was there with Henry Kissinger, setting up the president's upcoming visit. Recounting his experience, Reston wrote, "The hospital is an intensely human and vibrant institution ... like everything else in China these days, it is on its way toward some different combination of the very old and the very new." Having had acupuncture myself in 1973, I recall envisioning a growing exchange of Western science and philosophy with ancient tradition. Indeed, following the president's visit, scholars in both the arts and the sciences soon began to have access to previously hidden texts of spiritual classics. Translations of the *I Ching* and Lao Tsu's classic on Taoism, the *Tao Te Ching*, became easily available. And Joseph Needham's extraordinary study, *Science and Civilization in China*, published in 1956 and comprising tens of thousands of pages in many volumes, was added to the reference section of many libraries. While pouring over Needham's work one afternoon at the University of Cincinnati, I came across a section in Volume 2 on how the ancient Chinese used certain tools derived from the *I Ching* to locate the most auspicious site for building. The sages believed that many factors needed to be considered when choosing a site for a house, wrote Needham, but that "the forms of hills and the directions of watercourses, being the outcome of the molding influences of winds and waters, were the most important." This art of geomancy was called *feng shui* (literally, winds and waters) and was still widely practiced in many parts of the Far East. Much of its focus was on understanding an invisible energy called *chi* that permeates all living things. "The force and nature of the invisible currents... had to be considered." And one of the tools used, a compass called a *luo pan*, contained references to the building blocks of the *I Ching* and their arrangement, a "map" called a *bagua*. This map, again, showed the pattern of the magic square!

I searched for more information, finding copies of a wide variety of works on geomancy and the Chinese concept of invisible energy. I came across references to books with titles like *The Golden Box of Geomancy, Terrestrial Conformations for Palaces and Houses, Kuan's*

Geomantic Indicator, The Yellow Emperor's House-Siting Manual, Mysterious Principles of the Universe, and *Agreeable Geomantic Aphorisms.* Most works dated back to the third century BCE. After leaving college in 1971, I lived in Europe, where I soon became a serious student of the Unifying Principle, the *I Ching,* and feng shui. Encountering a group of Asian teachers who had begun their studies in Tokyo with the Japanese philosopher Georges Ohsawa, my attention shifted to matters of diet and health, and I became a practitioner of the way of life called "macrobiotics." By the mid-1980s, I was already lecturing on Nine Star Ki, the remarkable system of astrology developed from the *I Ching* and first introduced to me a few years before by Michio Kushi. I designed the offices and educational center where I offered classes entirely on the principles of feng shui. Visitors always commented favorably when they arrived—it was truly a remarkable space, designed in an octagonal shape and containing elements of magic and harmony no one could ever quite describe in words. I began to offer my design ideas, based on my studies and my intuitive understanding of feng shui and the Unifying Principle, to others setting up retail businesses, offices, homes, and apartments. A drawing board was soon visible in the corner of my office, and graph paper was evident everywhere. A series of courses I offered on the *I Ching* and Nine Star Ki was enormously well received, and I began to develop seminars in the United Kingdom, Europe, and Canada as well as expanding a series of seminars in the United States. At the same holistic retreat center where I'd taught my seminars the year before, a course was offered by Professor Yun Lin, a feng shui practitioner of the Tantric Black Sect of Tibetan Buddhism.

I watched feng shui students in amazement as they completely abandoned their own sense of aesthetics and design in favor of the Eastern motifs so frequently presented in Yun Lin's seminars. During consultations in New York or London, I came across a number of cases in which "cures" employed to correct design imbalances directly conflicted with the culture and surroundings of the occupants. Small tin wind chimes were hung in apartments decorated with modern Italian furniture; bamboo flutes, placed at forty-five-degree angles under heavy beams, contrasted with Chippendale tables. Artifacts from Chinatown, purchased for less than ten dollars, were hung near walls holding portraits worth millions painted by Dutch masters. Magic mirrors, red cloths, envelopes, and boxes were being carefully positioned under beds to attract money and improve health. No wonder people were confused, and put off, by what was available on feng shui in print. Something was very strange about the way things were being interpreted.

Similarly, students of Michio Kushi would often abandon their common sense and practice something quite different from what he was actually advocating. Caught in their own dogma, students of macrobiotics—like the followers of feng shui in the seminars I'd observed—would soon get into trouble. It was clear to me that the principles behind both macrobiotics and feng shui were not culturally specific to the Far East. I had encountered many other teachings on geomancy, architectural design, medicine, and health from Asia, Africa, northern Europe, and South America that never referred to feng shui or macrobiotics but were exactly the same practices. Although these disciplines offered the same foundation principles originating in a holistic cosmology, they were simply unrecognized in the West.

Soon, I began to see clients who were well known in business, entertainment, or the arts. My exploration of Tibetan Buddhism revealed to me more about the origin of feng shui and its use in environments where people were dying. Following an intensive training course with the Elisabeth Kübler-Ross Center in Virginia, I expanded my practice further to include spiritual care for the dying.

The world of "life force," or chi, became a very real experience in my life as I watched many people pass from this world. In the late 1980s, I began to expand my seminars to include a view of the "big life"—the real definition of macrobiotics—and in it, the study of human beings and their environments, their houses, and the spaces where they work and live. Despite having read about feng shui, most students who attended my seminars seemed to have no real understanding of how they could change their own environments and lives. All kinds of people—florists, bankers, storeowners, lawyers, consultants, real estate agents, actors, farmers, architects, and interior designers—began to seek my advice. Asked to consult on large projects, like the redesign of the world headquarters of an international bank and a central plaza of a European capital, I was challenged to go beyond tin wind chimes and bamboo flutes. What I offered, it seemed, was working, as new clients appeared in a steady stream.

I continued to offer seminars over the next few years, and one thing became very clear to me: These principles work. Hundreds of messages from students attested to the success they had gained as a result of making changes they learned about at the weekend seminars. Stories of improving relationships, healthy children, and new jobs were common. More than a few miracles showed up in the mailbox, and students taking the intermediate courses I developed stood up in front of total strangers to tell their own stories of transformation. People approached me at breaks and after lectures, whispering the most extraordinary tales of change in their lives following the course. Most asked when I'd write a book.

Feng Shui Made Easy was created after a lifetime of solving puzzles. Making the most complicated things more accessible and easily understood was bred into me; transforming philosophies and concepts into practical methods had been fascinating to me since childhood. This book will be like a feng shui consultant coming into your own home. *Feng Shui Made Easy* tells you more than just how to rearrange your furniture; it tells you how to change your life—and that is what feng shui is really all about. This is a remarkable system for self-development and a practical tool for improving business and relationships. All you need to do is practice—the energy flows by itself (there is nothing new under the sun and this information is no exception). I am simply trying to present it clearly and with some personal insights. I have "reorganized" this timeless message, like furniture in a room or articles on a desk, so that the reader can begin to grasp the whole rather than just the many parts. I employ the verb "to feng shui" in a lot of what I do these days. Used in this way, feng shui can mean "to harmonize, bring into balance, organize in a natural pattern," rather than carry with it the mystifying superstition imposed on it by those who cannot understand what they cannot measure and see. This book, in fact, "feng shuis" feng shui. This body of knowledge is not a tangent of mysticism extracted from an ancient culture's wisdom; it is the very heart of an understanding of life and integrates the vital system on which all of us must depend: our environment.

This book will introduce you to Intuitive Feng Shui®—a way that could quite accurately be called "vital design." It looks broadly at patterns over which we have absolutely no control, like the design of our solar system, and deeply into our own microcosms, down to the molecules of DNA. The Unifying Principle, the unspoken backbone of ancient culture and religion, links it all together. Most books about design and placement teach the reader *what*. This book is intended to add *how* and find out *why* and, in doing so, add a bit of magic to your life. Enjoy!

Chapter 1

A New Way of Being

Empty vessels make the most noise.

Sixteenth-century proverb

How to Read This Book

You have in your hand an instruction manual for creating and designing *living spaces.* Understanding one of the most important concepts of feng shui depends most of all on your ability to pretend (if necessary) that you know nothing and to observe your room and workplace from *emptiness.* Achieving this state of objectivity need not be difficult; we have all had moments when the slate was clean and we were open to any possibility. Recovering this perspective in order to look at our own homes or work areas requires a bit of practice; for some it may be easy, for others, a real challenge.

If you keep doing what you've done before (in the past), you will keep getting (in the future) what you've always gotten. Something has to change, and with feng shui you have the opportunity to begin to relate to the outer world as if it were a reflection of the inner psyche. Symbols appear everywhere in our environment; indeed, to the trained eye, your space reveals much more about who you are than you might like! Physiognomy, or face reading, and handwriting analysis are similar disciplines used to diagnose personality, but our faces and our handwriting are extremely difficult for us to change. Moving the position of a desk or changing the color of a wall is much easier and has far-reaching consequences, whether we are aware of them or not.

Feng shui is too powerful to ignore and too important to trivialize. In order to get the most from this book, read and study as much of the early chapters and exercises as you can *before* making any changes. Explore the invisible world in Chapter 2. Reflect on the power of feng shui and its potential in your life in Chapter 3. Establish your priorities as you are guided in Chapter 4. Become familiar with the *I Ching* in Chapter 5—it's easier than you think! Invite some friends over and fill in the First Impressions Worksheet in Chapter 6. Make sure you accurately place the key to feng shui, called the *bagua,* as detailed in Chapter 7. Look at your own house again, using the guidelines in Chapter 8. Look at your life again through the eyes of feng shui in Chapter 9. Then what you do will be grounded in understanding. What happens when you place a cure will result from what *you* create.

Chapters 10 through 13 introduce the cures in feng shui and will help the reader to make long-lasting, positive changes at home. If you have children, or want to learn more about the use of feng shui in their world, use the valuable insights in Chapter 14 to benefit future generations. If you are concerned about where you work, see Chapter 15, which has plenty of tips about the office environment. Those concerned with toxicity in the environment will want to look at Chapter 16 to learn about sustainable design and ecology from a feng shui perspective. Chapter 17 is a good overview of macrobiotics that can be useful to most readers. And everyone concerned about health, young and old, will gain a new point of view after reading the concluding chapter on feng shui and health.

Getting Started

If you are interested in the ordinary, then shopping in a store with decorators on staff may suit your needs. You may need to have them develop a particular style for you or pick the fabrics that from their viewpoint match other elements in your space. Perhaps you are concerned with being "in vogue," like the couple who worried that the renovation of their home would not be completed before the bleached white flooring they had chosen went out of style. Or maybe you are the design equivalent of being "tone deaf" in music and have no eye or taste that you can trust to be pleasant—let alone appropriate—without the guidance of a professional or an experienced friend. Recognizing the vast range of possibilities, you may be overwhelmed with information on design and balance and not feel well enough informed to practice feng shui without making a "mistake."

To get started, you may need to go backward. In the early days of offering seminars on feng shui, we handed out black plastic trash bags to participants as they left to go home. A few clever students turned that simple act into a movement, demonstrating that clearing clutter, simplifying your life, and creating hallowed space inside the home can make a huge difference. Washing those dusty slipcovers or throwing out that box of old belts and shoes in the hall closet is what we all must do before the magic can take hold. Plan to get a little dirty at first and work up a sweat. Spring cleaning has just begun—regardless of the season!

Find a clear and orderly space to sit and read further, and make yourself comfortable. As Lao Tsu told us, the longest of journeys begins with a single step.

Transformation

The world is ruled by letting things take their course. It cannot be ruled by interfering.

LAO TSU, *TAO TE CHING*

Who you need to be to practice this remarkable philosophy is simply someone who recognizes *possibility.* Anything can happen, and you are not limited by your design experience, taste, belief system, bank account, or expectations. Energy flows by itself; changes occur on their own. Miracles happen. In effect, what you will learn to do is to get out of your own way. We are always in the process of creating our future lives and destinies—nothing is already decided. Feng shui embraces free will and allows you to write the next chapter of your life. Some people refer to possibility as a "dream" and in so doing, limit themselves.

How you need to be is open. Possibility does not exist unless you are willing to consider it. When someone says "I love you," you must have a response other than "That's impossible!" It requires no belief to begin to live this way—just the smallest opening or space in which possibility can develop. Many times, people who begin to practice feng shui do not believe what happens, and that's fine. A new relationship or job comes along, shortly after they make some changes, and they tell their friends, "I can't believe this is happening! I bet this would have happened even if I *hadn't* made those changes!" Is it important to believe in something?

Georges Ohsawa, the Japanese philosopher who introduced macrobiotics to the West, taught a spirit of "noncredo"—one that is helpful to nurture. He felt that anything can happen (and does) according to basic laws in the universe that have more to do with the world of invisible spirit than the material world. When something does occur, you will *know* it, even if you still don't believe it, and you will begin to recognize the difference.

Setting Goals

Self-understanding is one of the main purposes
of philosophy—to understand the relationships
of men, things and words to each other.

ISAIAH BERLIN,
CONVERSATIONS WITH ISAIAH BERLIN

What do you want to change? Some who use this book will want to improve their lives, incomes, and relationships; others, after years of difficulty and a long stream of "bad luck," may need total makeovers. Setting some goals at the beginning of this practice will help you to gain a perspective of your life now, as well as evaluate the inevitable changes that occur later.

GOAL-SETTING EXERCISE

Turn a blank sheet of paper sideways so that it is like a landscape spread out in front of you. Imagine that it is divided into four equal quadrants.

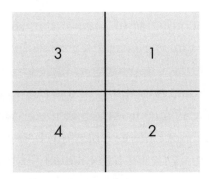

In the upper-right quadrant (1), write four words or phrases that best characterize your *current situation*. They can be positive or negative—"unemployed, angry at Mom, broke, stuck in a rut" or "reflective, busy all the time, feeling blessed, happily married." Any combination of positive, negative, or neutral words or phrases is fine. Be succinct and clear—don't take up the whole space.

Next, in the lower-right quadrant (2), write three or four positive words or phrases as goals you would like to achieve in three months. Put them down as declarations: "I will get a new job," or "My Mom and I will resolve our differences and support each other," or "My income will increase from new business contacts." *Make up your own goals!* Avoid goals like "I will win the lottery" or "I will marry a billionaire heiress." (Wait until you are sure you'd really want to.) Be reasonable!

Finally, write down three long-term goals (one year) in the upper-left quadrant (3). These could be much more lofty, like "I will embark on a whole new career path" or "I will marry the man of my dreams." Take a chance and be a bit *un*reasonable! In the final quadrant (4), write the words "The past is over."

Putting Feng Shui in Your Life

More than just the practice of geomancy, placement, or spatial arrangement, feng shui is primarily a philosophy and a unique way of seeing the world. It is important at the start to be both inquisitive and flexible, asking how things fit together as you move toward an ability to see the whole; however, as understanding comes, it is essential not to put your life in feng shui. Doing so almost always results in the creation of a mechanical monster, one that sees life as a series of fixed pictures and set patterns—a sure and fast road to arrogance. As extraordinary as this philosophy may seem to you, put feng shui in your life only as a point of reference at the beginning rather than the sole operating system.

For example, an architect or designer can use feng shui *after* he or she has used the creativity and skill needed to do the job. Then, as if putting on a new pair of 3-D glasses, the creator can look at the drawings using feng shui as a guideline and see what changes might need to be made. Do not try to create the ideal using feng shui as the template, as it will surely affect the creativity you need to come up with a unique design.

So much of what has come to us from ancient cultures has become dogmatic and, as such, limiting. When used appropriately, feng shui provides us with unlimited possibility in life, constantly changing and flowing, never restricting, always guiding. Beware of a tendency at first to "know" more than you have experienced. Observe, reflect, and build on your personal involvement with your surroundings and their relation to your life. You will soon see that no one could possibly know your own truth better than you. Feng shui will become, like a trusted old friend, an invaluable resource of wisdom and inspiration that simply gives you a new way of seeing your life.

The worksheet on the next page can be used as a prelude to making design changes in your home or office. After completing the worksheet, you will have a clearer idea of which areas of your life you might change using feng shui.

SELF-EVALUATION WORKSHEET

In each of the nine sections, read the description, and then, in the four groups of phrases below it, find the one that comes closest to speaking your truth. Every phrase need not be exactly like one you might use. To keep track of your answers, circle a letter—A, B, C, or D—for each area on the Answer Form that follows the worksheet.

The Journey

1. How do you feel about the work you are doing? Is your job in the field you want it to be in? Are you fulfilled by your work and acknowledged by the people around you in relation to your work? Are you considering a career change? These questions all relate to the area of your life that feng shui calls *Water.*

Water has to do with your path, your journey, the flow, or *Tao,* of your life, as if you are in a boat, sailing along through the years. It is not just your present job: you may be an aspiring artist temporarily working as a waiter while you wait for your first big break. And it does not relate to your salary or paycheck as a measure of success. This question evaluates your place on the "river of life"—whether you feel safe in the boat, whether you are flowing with the tide, crashing into or gliding by the rocks.

A. Life flows along quite well. I'm on the right road. I'm doing the work I want to do. I feel acknowledged by my coworkers. I am satisfied with the work I do. I feel productive. I have a good job. I feel fortunate to be doing what I really want to do and enjoying it. I feel I'm sailing on a beautiful ocean liner!

B. As above, but less so.

C. As below, but less so.

D. I feel like a salmon swimming upstream—definitely against the flow. I do not have a job. I am working, but not doing what I want. I'm thinking about going into a whole new field. My résumé is out there, but I am not getting any calls. I don't like my job and am looking for a new one. I haven't had much luck in the workplace these days. Help! I'm drowning!

Relationship

2. How are your relationships with your friends, spouse, and colleagues? Are you single with an active social life, or are you isolated, finding it difficult to meet anyone? How is your marriage? Is it a fulfilling partnership? Are you considering separation? Recently divorced? Blissfully in love? Desperately seeking? These questions relate to the area of your life called *Earth.*

The meaning of this area is receptivity, the ideal state in which relationships develop. It has to do with all partnerships, close associations both platonic and professional, and marriage, though not just matrimony as such. This question looks at relationships in general, whether they are going along well or with great difficulty, whether there are a number of eligible choices or none.

A. My relationships are great. I get a lot of attention from my mate. My social life is very active. My spouse is wonderful. I meet new people every week who ask me out. I feel as if we are still on our honeymoon. The phone hardly ever stops ringing. I'm recently engaged.

B. As above, but less so.

C. As below, but less so.

D. My social life is a disaster. I've tried everything to meet my match, but there just doesn't seem to be anyone interested. I feel jinxed. I'm in the process of separating. I just moved to town and have found it very difficult to meet new people—one date is easy, but they never call back. I thought celibacy would be better than this. I'm thinking about taking vows!

Elders

3. How would you characterize your relationships with your parents? Do you have a meaningful relationship with a teacher, mentor, or elder whom you consider an important part of your life? Even if one or both of your parents are deceased, how do you carry the memory of your life with them in your mind today? This area of life is represented by the symbol for *Thunder.*

Like the resonating bass of thunder that comes before a rainstorm, this question also relates to the foundation or root that preceded you, the ancestors who came before you and, in particular, your mother and father. It corresponds to our concern for family, parents, elders, teachers, and those in a superior position, such as your supervisor.

A. I get along very well with both my parents. I had a special relationship with one of my grandparents. My boss at work is a great supervisor. I have a mentor from college with whom I still keep in touch. I have a lot of teachers I highly respect. My dad died a while back; we finally came to peace over a lot of unresolved issues before he passed on. I'm grateful for so much my parents gave me. I have a deep respect for my ancestors.

B. As above, but less so.

C. As below, but less so.

D. I haven't spoken to my parents in years. My grandfather was a horrible man, and I never liked him. My boss is mean and insensitive. My mom and I argue all the time. My teachers never liked me. I don't usually get along very well with old people. One or both of my parents never really loved me very much. Don't ask!

Fortunate Blessings

4. How often in your life do you feel blessed? Is money a real problem for you? Are you terribly concerned with your bank account? Do you have positive cash flow, or are you always in debt? Do you feel fortunate, or are you on a seemingly endless streak of bad luck? This area of life feng shui calls *Wind*. It generates the energy of blessings from the material world—not just in hard cash but also in the general sense of fortune or "good omens" creating a state of auspiciousness. The wind brings good luck in the form of fortunate blessings from the material world.

A. I feel blessed with good fortune nearly every day. I make money and have a good income. People call me lucky. Money is really not a problem for me. Things show up just when I need them.

B. As above, but less so.

C. As below, but less so.

D. I'm broke. I could barely pay my rent last month. I do not have a job. I'm pretty far in debt right now. When it comes to luck, I'm having a bad streak these days. It's really hard to pay the bills recently. Blessed? Ha! How 'bout cursed!

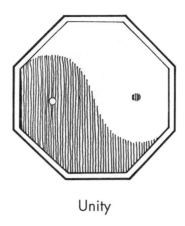

Unity

5. The central number five, located in the middle of the cardinal numbers one through nine, relates to the area of life called the *Tai Chi*. Regarded as the center of the universe, the Tai Chi is the place where heaven and earth meet and divide, creating the very breath of life force and all the other elements. There is no direct way to evaluate this area other than as a sum of the parts, because the Tai Chi has a part of every one of the eight other energies in it. A special section in Chapter 18 talks in greater detail about the significance of this central area as it relates to health.

Helpful Friends

6. Do you have a lot of close friends or helpers you can depend on in a crisis? Do you consider yourself helpful to others? Are you generous and supportive with your time and money, serving either as a volunteer, donor, or patron to a group less fortunate? Are there lots of people in your life who show up as helpful friends or "angels" of the visible and invisible type? This area of our lives is symbolized by the word *Heaven* and relates in the broadest sense to philanthropy.

Like a gift from heaven, the selfless acts of volunteers, friends, and "angels" in our lives are beyond measure; at the same time, our efforts as helpful friends in the unconditional service of others is truly one of life's greatest blessings.

A. I am an active volunteer in many organizations, giving both my time and money whenever I can. Many friends would do anything for me, as I would for them. Sometimes I feel I have a guardian angel watching over me. I try to give generously to those in need. A lot of people have helped me in times of trouble. I am amazed that, whatever you give, you always receive much more in return.

B. As above, but less so.

C. As below, but less so.

D. When I'm down and out, I'm on my own. I'd like to help others more, sure, but I'm just so busy and I barely get by myself. People don't usually think of me as someone to depend on for support. I don't see many volunteers that help our group. Everyone is in it for the money. Giving unconditionally is impossible. UFOs are all a government plot. There is no such thing as an angel except in fairy tales.

Creativity

7. Are you creative? Do you have children? How are your various projects going? Do you have writer's block, or do the ideas seem to pour out onto the paper? As a parent, is your relationship with your offspring rich and joyful, or full of turmoil and sadness? This area of life corresponds to the image of the *Lake*.

Here, the energy of creativity gathers, making possible the children, ideas, and projects to which we give birth and all that springs forth from the deepest internal spring that feeds our lives. The joy and beauty we see in all that we create is characterized by this open energy, like our children emanating a great depth of spirit.

A. My children are everything to me. I am very creative. I have no shortage of ideas or projects. Kids are great, and even though I don't have any, I really love them. As an artist, my creativity is my life, and I am very fortunate to be blessed with lots of it.

B. As above, but less so.

C. As below, but less so.

D. Children should be seen, not heard. I haven't had a new idea in years. We're having trouble conceiving. I can write poetry—if rhyming words counts—but usually I feel pretty blocked. The last big project I worked on failed miserably. I want kids, but I think I'm infertile. My children and I don't get along at all. I feel less creative than a block of wood.

Contemplation

8. What is your relationship with the spiritual world? Do you meditate, pray, or chant regularly? Are you an atheist, an agnostic, or a devout skeptic? Are you an active member of your church or temple, attending regular services and observing religious holidays? Our capacity for inner stillness is called the *Mountain* and signifies meditation, contemplation, and introspection.

It is not necessarily about organized religion or beliefs but relates more to our sense of the sacred and spiritual in life, often felt most strongly in the solitude of a mountain or cave where we can tune into ourselves.

A. My life is full of spiritual meaning. I meditate every day. I love reading scripture and teachings of the masters. I am religious in my own way. I've done a lot of searching in this area, through many avenues, and have gone through lots of changes. Life is a mystery.

B. As above, but less so.

C. As below, but less so.

D. I'm pretty skeptical about what science can't prove. I'd like to meditate, but I'm too busy. Books on religion and the "spiritual world" bore me. I used to believe in God, but when I see all these religions fighting with each other, I'm not so sure. What you see is all there is; the rest is all manufactured for mass consumption. The New Age is a marketing ploy. Prayer makes no difference in my life. God is dead. I don't understand this part.

Illumination

9. Do you care what other people think of you? Are you recognized in your field for the work you do? Are you fulfilled in life, or is there something still missing? Do you feel that all the answers to your problems are inside you, or do you need the guidance of others who "know" more? If you learned that you might die very soon, how do you suppose your life would change? The final area concerns the energy of *Fire* and relates to illumination or enlightenment.

Sometimes referred to—inadequately—as Fame, this area is more than just reputation or prominence; it has to do with the light that shines within. As the time comes when our lives draw to a close, we will understand more fully the meaning of enlightenment, as we grow closer to an inner brightness often present in the eyes of an elder sage. So, although the spotlight of media attention can make a movie star or a politician into a household name, being in the light is more about illumination within than public recognition.

A. Every day is another miracle. Sometimes life feels like dream. I have a good sense of myself and do not live to please others. I am usually very clear about my direction in life. People find me a source of inspiration. I feel contented to be alone, even though I enjoy other people in my life, too. My good intuition is a sign of my clarity.

B. As above, but less so.

C. As below, but less so.

D. How others feel about me matters a lot. I feel confused about half the time. Someone will show me how. Nobody really respects me for the work I do. It will be a long time before I'm anywhere near enlightenment. Death is a terrifying concept to me, and I am not ready, no way, not yet, please. Yeah, sure, His Holiness the Dalai Lama and me are good buddies—*not!*

SELF-EVALUATION ANSWER FORM

Circle your answers on this form before moving on to the next section.

Water	1.	A	B	C	D
Earth	2.	A	B	C	D
Thunder	3.	A	B	C	D
Wind	4.	A	B	C	D
Tai Chi	5. See Chapter 18				
Heaven	6.	A	B	C	D
Lake	7.	A	B	C	D
Mountain	8.	A	B	C	D
Fire	9.	A	B	C	D

Putting Your Priorities into Perspective

Once you have completed the Self-Evaluation Worksheet, it should be easier to see the areas in your life that are the most important to approach with feng shui. If, for example, you circled *D* under Thunder and *C* under Lake and *A* or *B* for the other areas, then these are the priorities that will need to be addressed in your living environment. The spaces around us reflect our inner worlds, so it is very likely that when you identify the actual areas of your house ruled by the energies of Thunder and Lake, you will see ways to change and improve this part of your living (and working) space.

Exactly what to do with this information will depend upon your ability to begin to relate to the invisible world of energy around you in much the same way you have explored the vibrational and emotional world within. An additional worksheet in Chapter 4 will guide you in doing just that.

Chapter 2

A Language for
the Invisible World

Look, it cannot be seen—it is beyond form.
Listen, it cannot be heard—it is beyond sound.
Grasp, it cannot be held—it is intangible.
These three are indefinable;
Therefore they are joined in one.

LAO TSU, *TAO TE CHING*

What Is Feng Shui?

Feng Shui is the art of adapting residences of the living and dead to cooperate and harmonize with the local currents of the cosmic breath.

ENCYCLOPEDIA OF CHINA, 1917

As modern society begins to discover traditional medicine, scientists and medical researchers continue to broaden their focus by considering the effect of the environment on individual health and well-being. The fields of building design and construction have already been radically changed by studies showing that potentially toxic elements are used in many common building materials. Background radiation emitted by high-tension wires, radar guns, or other sources, documented as a contributing cause of some cancers, is now a serious concern. Investigations into the effects of color and light on human behavior have helped many interior designers create healthier and more productive environments for the home and workplace.

The integration of the outside world and our internal environments is a cornerstone of most traditional philosophies. The Japanese saying *Shin do fu ji* (literally, soil and man not two) reminds us of the unity of human beings and the earth. Indigenous people all over the globe have always understood that we are not separate from our planet, our homes, or one another. Through in-depth study of the principles of unity and observation of the timeless, perfect order in the universe, feng shui brings together the external and internal environments by creating balanced, peaceful dwellings whose occupants can develop health and happiness.

In Asia in the earliest times, masters of the art of placement were originally employed to locate the most auspicious site for the tomb of a departed loved one. After the family selected the general area, the feng shui master would arrive with a *luo pan*, or geomancer's compass, and locate a site perfectly situated between mountain ranges, near the bend of a river, or in a valley where the ancestral spirits could be in harmony with heaven and earth. A tomb would be built there and blessed, and the family's good fortune would be enhanced by the effect on future generations of the properly cared-for spirit.

Luo pan compass

Over time, this classical practice of feng shui grew to include detailed observation of the living world and the way in which earth's energy affects all of daily life. Good feng shui meant prosperity and long life—a conscious connection between the outside environment and the world within. Considered part of the philosophy of the *I Ching,* feng shui remained an integral part of daily life until Western influences and political change began to erode this long-held, deep appreciation for the invisible.

The World of Vibrations

The gentle wind does move, silently, invisibly.
WILLIAM BLAKE

All matter is formed from vibration. Referred to as *chi* by the Chinese, *ki* by the Japanese, and *prana* or *brahman* by the peoples of India, this invisible electromagnetic energy radiates in particular patterns from objects of all shapes and sizes. Detailed maps of chi in the body reveal pathways of energy called meridians and form the basis of the practice of acupuncture and shiatsu massage therapy.

In an amputee's experience known as phantom pain, a knee itches that is not there to itch. Even though the whole leg has been removed, the energy that created it still remains. This phenomenon can be demonstrated through the use of Kirlian photography. A picture of a leaf using a Kirlian camera shows the "energy" of the leaf radiating from its edges. Cut off a corner of the leaf, and a new picture will still show the energy of the whole leaf, even though a part is now missing in the material plane.

This invisible energy, this vibration, flows constantly through all life forms. It has been closely observed and carefully detailed in the seven energy chakras observed in Ayurvedic medicine and the acupuncture meridians detailed in traditional Chinese medicine—both for thousands of years. Our earth has similar meridians, called ley lines, and concentrated power points that even in relatively recent times were acknowledged as places of great energy and spirit, where great cathedrals and shrines were erected by our ancestors. A day spent in Avebury, a small village in Great Britain where early inhabitants erected huge stone monoliths reflecting the movements of the sun and moon in relation to the earth, should convince most skeptics of the significance of this energy. It is a site of incredible power, where this energy is intensely focused; indeed, all over the globe, these sites are now being explored and appreciated for their potential healing qualities. Although recognized long ago, these qualities are now all but forgotten, with so much attention being paid to technology and material gain.

Divination

The geomancer's compass, the divining tool employed by the classical master, displayed the eternal pattern of the spiral, which reflected the infinite movement of chi between heaven and earth.

After positioning the eight or more rings to align with the directions, rivers, or mountain ranges, the feng shui master could detect blockages or surges of chi much as a dowser does using a divining rod or an acupuncturist using pulse diagnosis. The geomancer would then make suggestions for the shape or orientation of a dwelling and the placement of entryways and other design features, such as the location of bedrooms or kitchens, for the most harmonious environment. An astrological analysis of the occupants was studied because many decisions would depend upon the inhabitants' occupations, the proposed use of the rooms, and the overall understanding of the more subtle aspects of the invisible world.

Intuitive Feng Shui®

Although the art of placement is still widely practiced in some parts of Asia, the classical school employing the geomancer's compass is less evident in the West. In its place, *Intuitive* Feng Shui is fast becoming popular among designers, architects, and many in the healing arts who acknowledge the relationship between environment and health. Rooted in a universal cosmology like Eastern philosophy, Intuitive Feng Shui can help you learn how to practice "acupuncture in space." The success of this practice depends upon the clarity and understanding of the designer—you—based on your experience rather than your knowledge. Where there are blockages, practitioners can open pathways for energy flow by making various adjustments—just as in acupuncture. In order to activate or sedate energy, the practitioner carefully scrutinizes colors, shapes, textures, patterns, and materials, much as your diet would be reviewed as a factor affecting your internal environment.

This practice also relies on an understanding of the arrangement of space detailed in the ancient Chinese oracle known as the Book of Changes, or the *I Ching*, which is believed to have emerged as far back as 5,000 years ago. If it is used as a point of reference in the design process, architects using feng shui can create extraordinarily powerful structures, setting the stage for the occupants' good fortune. Many frequently imitated modern architects remain on the cutting edge due, in part, to the great advantage this profound wisdom brings. However, a building that looks similar to one created using feng shui principles, but is designed without an understanding of the whole, can easily create a nightmare for its occupants.

Intuitive Feng Shui is distinguished from the classical approach by the practitioner's focus on instinct, feeling, and intuition. These three forces, constantly at work in every individual, are the precise source of the inherent wisdom that created the cosmological philosophies of all ancient cultures. Rather than trying to analyze and interpret complex systems of energy or culturally specific directives from another time and place, the practitioner of Intuitive Feng Shui learns to uncover the ever-present wisdom *within*. Changes are made based on clarity, judgment, and the elusive storehouse of intuition to which we all have direct access. Interestingly, the Japanese characters for the word *intuition* mean, literally, "original ability."

Feng shui actually has less to do with the external world than with our infinite inner space, which is the awareness of our consciousness beyond the confines of time and space. The aim of the practice of feng shui is to free up blockages of energy to allow possibility, to create harmony and bring balance between all complementary opposite forces—especially the internal and external worlds. Intuitive Feng Shui is much more about clearing the path for energy to flow than about "getting more" and can open space that we may think is not even there. We choose to live inside the structures of our homes in time and space, but the more we can incorporate the wisdom of the bigger picture, the more in touch with life we become.

Recognizing the dichotomy between "getting more" and "letting energy flow" sheds light on two different ways feng shui can be practiced. One way, which has become increasingly popular, is often referred to as "power feng shui"—achieving as much power, money, and personal well-being as possible, regardless of what happens to anybody else. The inner mantra of consultants who use power feng shui is "What's in it for me?" The idea is to amass as much good fortune as possible, manipulating environments in order to win, with no regard for a neighbor or business that may be left downwind, in the shadow, or with an obstructed view of the landscape.

Power feng shui fits right in with the competitive paradigm that has led to the increasing destruction of our planet and our inner tranquility. Human beings become increasingly isolated from the environment in the same way that conventional medicine looks at a part of the body while taking little interest in who you really are inside. This approach fails to recognize that the part and the whole are different but inseparable configurations, or patterns, of the same energy.

If feng shui is used only for external applications, its original nature—the alignment of internal spirit and an understanding of the architecture of consciousness and being—is disregarded. Forgetting this, we live in illusion. Aware that feng shui emerged from the teachings of the *I Ching*, the heart of Taoism, which speaks to our inner world of being through the higher self, we are really exploring the spiritual dimensions inside us, the place where we can all experience our common unity. It operates from the realization that we are each a reflection of each other within a universal source and prompts us to ask, "How can we improve things for the benefit of all?" Practiced from this premise, Intuitive Feng Shui is a unique approach to *interior* design.

All approaches to feng shui ultimately present a view of the infinite world in which the ancients were able simply to *be*—to live in awareness, with consciousness. Today there is the temptation to skip over or disregard the organization of our inner framework and have a second-hand, conceptual experience of ourselves from the outside, as if from an observer's point of view. Feng shui practiced this way is loaded with landmines waiting to detonate, namely the dogmatic adherence to concepts which were practiced by the ancient sages, but which we have not taken the time to assimilate by creating the experience within our own consciousness. It is the principles behind these teachings that lead us to look within and refine our internal chi.

Just like the knowledge required to repair a jet engine, these teachings are a great and fascinating body of knowledge that requires deep study and understanding. As with any purely technical application, the mechanics of feng shui are only as good as the technician. What's more, feng shui is about *living* energy, which requires more than data generated from a software package, or "dos and don'ts" memorized from books and workshops. After some time, you will become a more sensitive receiver of energy; therefore, information is only one part. As you start, you will often intuitively determine the source of a problem and make appropriate corrections—but the more weighed down you become by information on the "right" way to do things, the more this spontaneous quality is suppressed.

All lasting change comes from within. In order to be more at peace, we must open ourselves to the inner world and the workings of our higher being. This leads to action from conscious presence. As we awaken our original ability—our intuition—we find ourselves experiencing the world in its largest context and realize that it actually goes against our nature to narrow our focus only to the material plane. Your reawakening to the sacred in everyday life will imbue your feng shui practice with vitality and purpose.

We often experience the world as the result of the limitations of our consciousness, our past conditioning, the experiences of our childhoods, and our lower levels of learned behavior. To be able to hear above the noise generated by this accumulated psychic clutter, to open the way for our free intuition to awaken, we need to address our past "unfinished business" and clear it out. Our innate intuitive qualities are weakened by overindulgence, eating on the run, stress, fatigue, arrogance, a compulsive obsession with information, and an excessive focus on the material world.

What is most often called "intuition" is really an inner knowing. It is an instant of clarity, like a bolt of lightning from heaven, a direct email from the universe, without question. Our intuitive genius is strengthened by "inner exercise"—the acceptance of knowing without guessing. As a kind of spiritual discipline, Intuitive Feng Shui might also include some useful practices such as fasting, chanting, meditating, laughing, yoga, Tai Chi, gardening, eating correctly, and chewing consistently. These can lead to a balanced life, cultivating an awareness of deep humility.

Chapter 3

Places of Power

A direct and superficial examination of things
does not always enable us to conclude that
reality is identical with perception.
PIERRE LECOMTE DU NOÜY, *HUMAN DESTINY*

A Bit of History

Some of the most extraordinary monuments of ancient life on earth can be found among the rolling hills of Great Britain just a few hours' drive from London. For those who have visited these unusual sites, Stonehenge, Avebury, and Silbury Hill are not easily forgotten—even though their significance may not have been fully understood. Scholars the world over have devoted thousands of hours of research and study to setting forth various theories of why these sites were constructed and what they might have meant to the inhabitants of our planet who designed and erected them.

It is agreed, however, that these landmarks are among dozens more in this region that fall along a perfectly straight line that one can easily see by examining a map of the area. No doubt the ancients were able to discern a concentration of some type of energy that ran through the region. That they erected monoliths, earthen mounds, temples, and church naves *precisely* on this line can hardly be written off as mere coincidence. Just what they were up to—the *why* of it all—is still in question.

The Forces of Heaven and Earth

Energy, or chi, is an effect of the force from either heaven or earth. It is always moving in the pattern of a spiral, and we can easily visualize it by observing phenomena on the planet from the point of view of astronauts in outer space. From amid the spiral of our own solar system, a look down at the planet Earth reveals swirling cloud patterns, the funnel clouds of hurricanes and tornadoes, and the movement of oceans. In the northern hemisphere, spiraling air currents most often rotate counterclockwise. Cross the equator, however, and the movement changes to clockwise—still spiraling, but in the opposite direction to movement above the equator.

As we look more closely at life on earth, we can see nature's expression of this pattern everywhere: the antlers of an elk, the design of tree branches, a form of a seashell, the structure of creation itself. In human beings, this emerging pattern begins with the movement of sperm and egg—in a spiral—and is imprinted in our bodies hundreds of times. Fingerprints, hair growth, esophageal lining, nerve fibers, sexual organs, cardiac tissue—it is in everything, down to the double helix of our most basic building block, the spiral of DNA.

This irrefutable pattern of the universe, manifesting from space (heaven's force) and from the earth itself (earth's force), is the expression of chi energy harnessed in prehistoric times with the building of monuments like Stonehenge and Silbury Hill. Modern technology now permits us to measure the intensity of this energy, validating—for skeptics, at least—the existence of something unusual on these sites.

Like Avebury nearby, Silbury Hill was placed by human beings to concentrate earth's force and in so doing attract more of heaven's force to the site. The monoliths placed in a particular pattern at

Stonehenge and Avebury are magnets to heaven's force, an act of acknowledging life itself. Here, no doubt, were festivals, celebrations, birthing rituals, observances of summer solstices and autumnal equinoxes enhanced by the proper placement of objects to intensify this vibrational field.

In contrast to this attracting of the living force of heaven, sites near Avebury and other sites on the Stonehenge Ley were used for quite a different purpose. One example, called the Longbarrows, is a long, cave-like tunnel, equally mysterious to most modern city folk, who try to understand what *is* there rather than what is *not* there.

The Longbarrows has quite a different energy present: it was designed and constructed to harness earth's force as it rises upward in the invisible world of chi. Inside the cave tunnel, small cubicles lead to a central "altar" where the ancients could take advantage of the intense concentration of the same force present when a human being's time on earth ends. Here, and in similarly charged locations throughout the world, our ancestors would sit to meditate, becoming one with the essence of their true nature and gracefully detaching from their physical form.

As we die, our final breath is inward and upward. These early astral travelers might have practiced in the outer cubicles and, when their time came to depart for the next world, taken their position at the altar and "blasted off" with the concentration of earth's force focused beneath them.

Not a cemetery, burial ground, or tomb of any sort, the Longbarrows was simply a place where life on earth would end and the physical form would be discarded. Even the Romans, at the foundation of their cities, constructed a vertical shaft with a rounded roof, not unlike Longbarrows, where the departed spirits might receive gifts from the living, ensuring a continuity of generations.

Making Conscious Choices

Though we may not be interested in creating an environment in our home or office that makes it possible to leave our body for astral travel, or to capture an energy appropriate for celebration of life, it is clear that such distinctly different activities can be enhanced through a careful understanding of the elements present in the environment to focus the force of heaven or earth. In fact, some bedrooms where occupants complain of insomnia have too much heaven's force—not because they are sited over a ley line or on top of a manmade mound, but because of the choice of colors, shapes, textures, patterns, and placement in the overall design. And some offices where workers commonly complain of fatigue are environments that feel more like a barrow—the result of architectural and interior design choices that were made unconsciously yet powerfully affect human behavior.

You are here

The practice of feng shui enables you to create environments suitable for their intended activity. It also empowers you to correct existing imbalances in order to improve your life. The understanding necessary to achieve these results, however, requires looking at the world in a completely different way—largely misunderstood in Western culture that focuses as much on what is not there as on what is there. Many people are so sure of their reality—so locked into seeing the world a certain way—that it is extremely difficult for them to leave behind a way of seeing the world that fits "the norm."

The Story of the Well Frog

Once upon a time, there was a frog that lived in a well behind a small house in the woods. One day, when the frog was hopping around his home, he came upon another frog, whom he had never seen before.

"Who are you—and where did you come from?" he asked the other frog.

"I am from the ocean," the new frog replied.

"The ocean? What is that like?" asked the Well Frog.

"It's big," said the Ocean Frog. "Big! How big? Is it as big as, say, a quarter of my well?"

"It is," the Ocean Frog quickly responded, adding, "even bigger...."

"Well, then! Is it as big as half my well?" asked the Well Frog, now with more confidence.

"Yes, my friend, it is even bigger than half!"

"Bigger still? Incredible! Can you show me this place where you live, this ocean you call home?"

"Of course," said the Ocean Frog, "but you'll have to leave the well and follow me!"

"OK, let's go there!" said the Well Frog and hopped up the stones on the side of the well to join his new friend.

The Ocean Frog led the way to the very top of the well, jumped off the edge into the dirt, and headed off through the woods. The Well Frog followed close behind. At the edge of woods, they came to a clearing, and the Ocean Frog, not hesitating, hopped through the open field and over another hill, until he came to a sandy beach. There, at the edge of the water, the Ocean Frog turned around as the Well Frog arrived. They sat and looked out over the ocean.

"See," said the Ocean Frog, "this is the ocean where I live."

Whereupon the Well Frog looked out into the vast expanse that lay in front of him and exploded.

Once we leave home (what we know) and go beyond the limiting factors (walls, borders, or boundaries), anything can happen! When you begin to perceive the power of the invisible world, you may very well explode, too—with possibilities for a new future!

Feng Shui in Today's Environment

What we don't know about life covers a lot more territory than what we do know. The world of architecture and building design has changed dramatically over the past twenty years, due in part to the explosion of technology, computer-aided design, and major advances in understanding the importance of energy conservation. We have only just begun to sense the consequences of all of this, identifying some buildings as sick, some environments as plastic or artificial, and some materials as toxic. The tip of the iceberg—or edge of the ocean, if you will—has finally been reached as we enter an age when we are more aware of the impact of the energy we can't so easily measure. Sustainability is being redefined.

As a society, we have reached a point where everything matters, from the microscopic to the supra global. Real, sustainable solutions such as those envisioned by inspiring global thinkers like Edward O. Wilson, Gunter Pauli, William McDonough, Simon Velez, Cameron Sinclair and many other cutting-edge scientists, system builders, designers, and advocates of permaculture are stimulating a new vision of blue and green economies, giving birth to new paradigms of design and reawakening a world where a truly sustainable future is genuinely possible. Chapter 16, "Feng Shui and Ecology," expands these ideas further.

Design that respects life and incorporates nature is a lot more than just a shopping mall with ramps for wheelchairs and lots of potted plants. Living design feels the way homemade bread smells: warm, delicious, and irresistible. Designers of the future may not turn their backs on computers but will, of necessity, use intuition, instinct, and creativity much more in order to build vital environments sensitive to the people who inhabit them. The understanding of energy flow, the forces of heaven and earth, sound waves, light, living objects, and personal health will become far more important to our happiness and very existence than fad, fashion, or facades. What underlies every space is the living energy all of us feel. This is feng shui today— not just "wind and water" from an ancient culture a thousand years ago but the creation of enduring, living spaces with fresh air and free flowing water. Reuniting with the majesty and timeless presence of the energy of planet Earth, feng shui provides a means to harmonize opposites: heaven and earth, man and woman, instinct and intellect, outer and inner, being and the Divine.

Chapter 4

Is There a Doctor in the House?

There was a crooked man, and he walked a crooked mile,
He found a crooked sixpence against a crooked stile:
He bought a crooked cat, which caught a crooked mouse.
And they all lived together in a little crooked house.

J. O. HALLIWELL

Diagnosis

Living in a crooked house will make your life full of crooked things. Because who you are, the way you perceive your life, and what's going on now will be revealed in your environment, the Self-Evaluation Worksheet can be assessed in different ways. In order to have some indication of where to look in your house, the first step in Intuitive Feng Shui is to ask questions about your life. If you scored all *A*s, then there is really no need at this time to get an *A*+. But because each part of the whole is related in some way to every other part, like paired organs in the body or the complementary, antagonistic relationships that appear throughout the natural world, correcting just one thing will affect everything else in your life. A warm relationship with our parents greatly improves our chances of finding happiness with a significant other; doing what we want to do in life positively affects our sense of the invisible world of spirit. Don't be concerned if your score contains a few letters other than *A*—or no *A*s at all!

Your Priorities List

The next step is to turn your Answer Form into a priorities list by writing down the numbers in descending order of score, leaving all *A*s off your list. Suppose the Answer Form for your self-evaluation looks like the example that follows.

SELF-EVALUATION ANSWER FORM

Water	1.	(A)	B	C	D
Earth	2.	A	B	C	(D)
Thunder	3.	A	B	C	(D)
Wind	4.	A	B	C	D
Tai Chi	5. HEALTH				
Heaven	6.	A	(B)	C	D
Lake	7.	(A)	B	C	D
Mountain	8.	(A)	B	C	D
Fire	9.	A	(B)	C	D

Your priorities list would then be 2, 3, 4, 6, and 9—Earth, Thunder, Wind, Heaven, and Fire.

On the positive side, this would indicate that you are doing what you want to do, are on the right road, have a great job or are satisfied with the journey and gave yourself an *A* in Water. You also have a good relationship with your children, or feel very creative, or are not concerned with offspring and scored yourself an *A* in Lake, too. And with matters of spirit, you also feel good—perhaps you meditate, or attend church regularly, or have a healthy perception of spiritual things that caused you to grade the area known as Mountain with an *A*.

When the questions about relationship were evaluated, however, you gave yourself a *D* in Earth—either because you are single (and don't like it), or were recently divorced or separated, or because you have a lot of negative feelings about your relationship, partnership, or marriage. Family issues pushed some buttons, too, in this example, as a score of *D* in Thunder reveals difficulty with your parents or elders, unresolved arguments with teachers, or some other challenge with those who came before you that carries a charge. Because Earth and Thunder both got *D*s, they go at the top of the priorities list in the order they appear. Wind, which was graded *C*, goes next, revealing some difficulty with money, blessings, and feelings of good fortune. Heaven and Fire, which you graded *B*, are placed last on the list in the order they occur. This example indicates only a small issue with helpful friends and self-enlightenment, significant enough to include them as areas to address, but less important than those that got *C*s or *D*s and not like those that do not need to appear on this list at all: those that received an *A*—Water, Lake, and Mountain.

This exercise requires you to make some distinctions in your life, to list in order, with some qualifications, the areas of your life that need the most attention. Your list may include all eight areas or only one—the number does not mean anything, because we all perceive our lives differently. The good news is that we can change things, and as we begin to clarify what needs changing, the priorities list helps us start to put our house in order.

What Needs Fixing?

The list 2, 3, 4, 6, 9 means the areas symbolized by the energies of Earth, Thunder, Wind, Heaven, and Fire in your house need correction, improvement, or change. No doubt you will need little convincing of this, because you've probably searched for a mate, read lots of self-help books about parents and children, and attended a few spiritual seminars or meditation classes before creating this list. But instead of addressing these issues directly, Intuitive Feng Shui will show you how to deal with them by changing your environment, the space in which you live your life.

Before examining your house and learning how to change it, it is important that you reflect on each of the areas on your priorities list. Go through each area of your life and visualize what you want it to look like—not just how it is. In all things, and in particular in Intuitive Feng Shui, *image* precedes *matter*. The world of vibration comes before the materialization of the physical world, so it is extremely helpful, regardless of your belief system, to imagine how things could be and to begin practicing what it means to consider *possibility*.

The following is only an example of what you might say. Let your own words speak your truth—don't just copy a phrase from the example. Be positive—consider even the possibility of a *miracle!*

Completing the Visualization Process Worksheet

On the worksheet provided, first write the number and house you are working on (for example, 2—Earth), and then you might write something like the following:

- I visualize a good man who is sensitive to my needs.
- I can see my partner, and I begin to accept our differences and focus more on how we complement each other.
- I am attracting women who start to notice me and accept my invitations to go out.

- I have more choices than I know what to do with!
- I see my mate forgiving me for the past, and we start to create a future again.

Then create a space for 3—Thunder. You might write

- I notice that my mother starts to care more about my opinions and stops acting as if she's the only one who knows anything.
- My feelings of anger and resentment over what my grandfather did turn into forgiveness, and I let go of all that bitterness in the past.
- I see a change in my boss, who stops complaining and actually appreciates something for a change.

In the space for 4—Wind, you might write

- I get a raise at work and I can pay off my debts.
- One of my poems is published in a national magazine.
- Finally, I win something—for the first time in my life!
- A streak of good luck comes my way—I feel so blessed.
- Looks as though I am finally in the right place at the right time.

In the space for 6—Heaven, you might write

- I can really count on Michael—he's a great friend.
- I see the people at work start asking me how they can help instead of always turning their backs on me.
- My neighbors and I start to take care of one another—following the Golden Rule.
- I recognize that I really do have a guardian angel! Incredible!

In the space for 9—Fire, you might write

- I'm not concerned with what other people think about me.
- The answers are all inside me.

- People are starting to be more attracted to me and are asking me for my opinion.
- I can begin to see that who I am never really dies.

Your own worksheet would contain phrases that you could imagine using if your life changed in the ways you want it to as a result of evaluating these areas sometime in the near future. They should be *I* statements, from your perspective, not "My father apologizes ..." but rather "I see my father..."

Keep this list so you can make the feng shui adjustments detailed later in the book. At the very least, each area should improve by one grade—and some may even become *A*s and fall off the list!

VISUALIZATION PROCESS WORKSHEET

1. Water (The Journey)

_____

_____

_____

_____

_____

_____

_____

_____

_____

_____

_____

_____

_____

_____

_____

_____

_____

_____

_____

_____

2. Earth (Relationships)

3. Thunder (Elders)

_____

_____

_____

_____

_____

_____

_____

_____

_____

_____

_____

_____

_____

_____

_____

_____

_____

_____

_____

_____

_____

_____

_____

4. Wind (Fortunate Blessings)

5. Tai Chi (Health)

6. Heaven (Helpful Friends)

7. Lake (Creativity)

_____

_____

_____

_____

_____

_____

_____

_____

_____

_____

_____

_____

_____

_____

_____

_____

_____

_____

_____

_____

_____

8. Mountain (Contemplation)

9. Fire (Illumination)

Chapter 5

Traditional Wisdom for Modern Times

The I Ching

Understanding feng shui intuitively rests upon many foundations, but none is more important than a working knowledge of the *I Ching*. This traditional oracle is said to have been first envisioned by Fu Hsi, the father of civilization, as far back as 5,000 years ago. As legend tells us, this sage was meditating one day by the banks of the Lo River in northern China when a tortoise emerged from the water. In a moment of divine inspiration, Fu Hsi realized that the entire universe was reflected in the orderly markings on the shell of the tortoise.

The Eight Trigrams

The configurations of solid and broken lines, arranged in threes, reflected the macrocosm using the microcosm of eight trigrams—all the possible combinations of three solid and broken lines. These eight markings symbolized every aspect of nature: Heaven, Earth, Fire, Water, Mountain, Lake, Wind, and Thunder. Furthermore, all emotions, physical matter, spiritual qualities—everything—could be ascribed to one of the eight trigrams. From this, Fu Hsi saw the Perfect World and laid down the abstract design known as the Lo Map Early Heaven Sequence. Reflective also of the nine cardinal numbers (where the middle number, five, has no specific trigram), the pattern he created was, perhaps, the original magic square.

The Book of Changes was created by combining these eight symbols in all possible ways, resulting in sixty-four chapters of wisdom on the nature of change. Passed on by word of mouth for centuries until writing was invented, this oracle was considered the most direct link to the human understanding of our place between heaven and earth. In 1200 BCE, two royal scholars, King Wen and the Duke of Chou, amplified the verses, producing a more detailed description close to the texts available today. They also changed the position of the eight trigrams on the Lo Map, creating a Later Heaven sequence that reflected not the Perfect World in an abstract form but a world in motion—changing—with human beings at the center. Five hundred years later, no lesser sages than Confucius and Lao Tsu would spend their whole lives studying its profound wisdom as an inexhaustible source of inspiration and spiritual guidance.

Today, there are as many as a hundred translations of the *I Ching* published in English, and thousands of other books and articles available, ranging from scholarly examinations of their cultural symbolism to simplistic fortune-telling guides for the market investor. Considered together with Lao Tsu's classic *Tao Te Ching* as the basis of Taoist philosophy, the *I Ching* remains a personal oracle that defies description or comparison with any other historical body of knowledge.

The arrangement of trigrams in the magic square, known as the Lo Map Later Heaven sequence, is used in Intuitive Feng Shui as the starting point from which all design decisions are made. The "grid"—or bagua—is the overlay on a plot of land, a house, or a room that the architect or designer balances using basic design principles. These employ color and light, ordinary corrections of geometric ratios, arrangement of space for harmonious flow of traffic, and a number of more esoteric solutions for important areas of the bagua that the occupants wish to enhance. In Chapter 7, a detailed explanation of the bagua and its use will enable you to open the door to this invisible pattern of energy.

The Bagua

Looking more closely at the Later Heaven Sequence that forms the basis of the bagua, it is possible to see a relationship between trigrams in pairs from both the physical placement and their energetic symbolism. The first "pure" pair is Heaven and Earth, signified by three solid lines ☰ and three broken lines ☷. This pair is known as the Universal Opposites. Next come the Organic Opposites, Fire ☲ and Water ☵; then come Mountain ☶ and Lake ☱, referred to as the Natural or Elemental Opposites; finally, there are Wind ☴ and Thunder ☳, called the Impulsive Opposites. This completes the four pairs, the eight trigrams of the bagua.

Universal Opposites		Organic Opposites		Elemental Opposites		Impulsive Opposites	
Heaven	Earth	Fire	Water	Mountain	Lake	Wind	Thunder

It is fascinating to observe that the structure of each trigram conveys a certain quality of energy closely associated with its symbolism. Heaven, made of three solid lines, is the creative force—the essential spirit from which all else manifests. Exactly opposite in composition is Earth, with its three broken lines, the receptive force, open to receive Heaven's blessing as the soil receives nourishment from the sun, rain, and other forces in the atmosphere around it. Together, they correspond also to the masculine and feminine.

Examining the trigram for Fire, you can see two solid lines above and below a broken line, appearing very much like the image of a flame. It looks as if there is form to a flame when, in reality, the core is empty. The trigram for Water, on the other hand, is made up of two broken lines on both sides of a solid line in the middle; although water appears to be clear and open, it does have mass at the center. The trigram for Mountain, a solid line above two broken lines, creates the image of space inside a container, like a cave in the side of a mountain; Lake is composed of the inverse arrangement, open on the surface, with mass below—much like a deep lake. Here, there is a distinction between Water and Lake: the former is open on both sides (like the path formed by running water) while the latter is seen more from the open top, closed at the bottom like a bowl. The last pair, the Impulsive Opposites, reveals images that are again very much like their names. The roaring bass of thunder is a powerfully solid force; as it rises, thunder disperses harmlessly. The trigram for Thunder contains an unbroken line at the base with two broken lines above. Wind has no root but carries a strong force over the ground; the trigram has a broken line below with two solid lines above it.

Fu Hsi observed images of the vibrational world in relation to the elements of nature. Other symbols that correlate with each trigram serve to reinforce these associations. Heaven, the creative force, supports and nourishes all that manifests on earth through human affairs; thus the house is called Helpful Friends. Earth, the receptive, stands for the greatest of all principles in any marriage—that of listening, receiving, and embracing every-

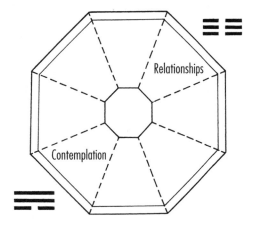

thing—unconditional love. This house is aptly called Relationships. Like every other pair, the Universal Opposites depend on each other and remain connected through the vibrational world. The house signified by the trigram for Fire refers to *internal* light and clarity, and so is called Illumination; Water, flowing through time like our everyday lives, is The Journey. Fire and Water have long been related in obvious ways; in the bagua, it is through entering our life at The Journey that we can finally arrive at self-realization, Illumination. The Mountain cave is the symbol of quiet introspection and meditation called Contemplation; it stands in relationship to our joyful expression in the outer world, through our offspring, and all that we manifest through this house, which is called Creativity. Thunder is like the booming voice of our predecessors, our superiors, and thus the house is called Elders; Wind is the constant flow of good fortune given by the gift of life itself; the house is called Fortunate Blessings.

Both physical and vibrational relationships exist in the bagua. Heaven is related in *image* to Earth, but *physically,* 180 degrees across the bagua, we see Mountain. Our relationships with others really emerge from our inner world; thus the correlation also exists between Relationships and Contemplation.

Fire and Water are in relationship through both the physical world and the world of image or vibration. Even when we achieve some fame or prominence, coming under the spotlight, what matters most is doing what we really want—honoring The Journey and its connection with Illumination.

The very life our parents and ancestors have given us is the greatest of all blessings; thus the inseparable relationship between Elders and Fortunate Blessings. As we come to terms with our elders, we can much more easily realize our self-expression through creativity and procreativity, our children. The images of Elders and Creativity are always connected within our psyche.

When we are blessed with good fortune, Wind will be in relationship with Heaven; what better can we do with all those bless-

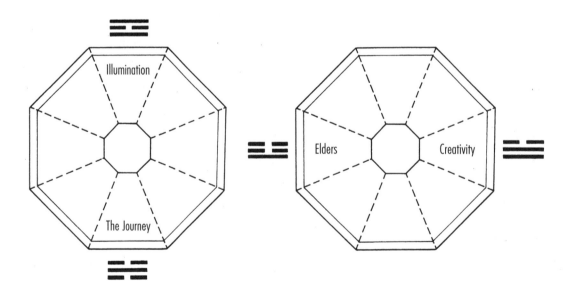

ings than to share them with others and live like Helpful Friends, the house directly across the bagua.

Step Back and Take a Look

When all of these houses are in balance, powerfully related through the polarity of their physical and vibrational forces, we are said to be in a state of harmony, the essence of feng shui. This image is signified by the Tai Chi, called Unity, closely related to our overall health. Although health is often thought to be merely the absence of sickness, *true* health from this perspective means good relationships with every house of the bagua: doing what we want to do with our lives (One—The Journey, Water); nourishing companionships or a vital marriage (Two—Relationships, Earth); feeling grateful and respectful appreciation for our parents, teachers, and ancestors (Three—Elders, Thunder); experiencing good luck and a sense of blessing in our everyday lives (Four—Fortunate Blessings, Wind); being in good relationship with many others who support us, and

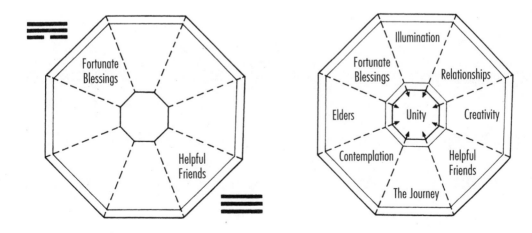

giving back through philanthropy to those who need our support (Six—Helpful Friends, Heaven); sharing ourselves with little or no effort through our own original expression (Seven—Creativity, Lake); taking time to meditate, be still, and look within as we embrace the miracle of life (Eight—Contemplation, Mountain); and realizing our true, divine nature (Nine—Illumination, Fire.) *All* houses of the bagua in harmony create Health (Five—Unity).

Take a moment to envision the whole. See how every house of the bagua has at least one other related house, through the physical and vibrational world. What occurs in our homes and workplaces is connected in the same way—through the pattern of these powerful, symbolic associations. Whether we are aware of it or not depends entirely upon our perspectives and the interpretations we make in every environment. In feng shui terms, clearly demonstrated in the integrity of the bagua and the Lo Map of the *I Ching,* life is not a random assembly of parts but a unified whole ruled by a pattern of the invisible world of energy.

Chapter 6

A New Way of Seeing

We see very largely with the mind, and only partly
with the eyes. The phenomenon of vision depends
upon the mind's interpretation of the impression
upon the retina. What we see is not that impression
but our own interpretation of it.

WILLIAM BATES, MD, *THE BATES METHOD*

The human body is like a massive electrical power station. Our nervous system, highly developed and uniquely integrated, is the ultimate computer—reliable hard drive, lightning-fast random memory, and instantaneous character recognition. Our senses, acting in harmony, record and process data that enables us to form nearly immediate impressions about our environment.

Of our sensory organs, none is more active than our eyes. The nervous system will use billions of receptors to process information; almost two-thirds of these are related to vision. When you are looking for the right house, a new car, or a special someone in your life, a picture is truly worth a thousand words. And your first impression may very well be most of the story.

The easiest way to change your life may just be by changing the places in which you live and work. In the same way that it is hard for us to truly see ourselves, we cannot know what impression our house or office has on others. It is helpful to have some objective input when evaluating our environment, so ask a few people to fill out the worksheet in this chapter. See how close what you think others notice is to what they actually see and experience. Like the squirrels and owls in the trees of a hidden-picture puzzle, that which is obvious to some may remain hidden from others.

First Impressions

A beautiful painting or a vase of fresh flowers in your front hallway may be obscured by the heavily worn, stained carpet that you've overlooked for years. It may be the carpet, though, that is your guests' first impression. The comfortable armchair you have positioned in front of your desk for visitors may go unnoticed, competing with the cold, abstract marble sculpture in the corner behind you that is immediately visible to people entering your office. Intending to make the space feel warm, open, and safe for your clients, you create the opposite first impression. The fixed, powerful statement made by the art actually overshadows the more giving aspects of the furniture, causing those who visit to experience what takes place in this environment as rigid, insensitive, and impersonal.

On a hot summer day, the simple *sound* of running water in a fountain, bathtub, or waterfall gives us such a distinct impression of coolness that subjects in one study estimated the temperature in a room to be an average of eight degrees lower than it actually was compared with the same room with no running-water sounds.

What we *smell* has a deep effect on our behavior too. According to the experience of hundreds of real estate agents, the aroma of freshly baked bread or homemade cookies will do almost as much to sell a house as a new coat of paint on the front door. Fresh lilacs or honeysuckle blossoms on the path leading up to the front door bring a smile to the faces of all but the highly allergic. By contrast, garlic, the compost pile, or the family pet may smell like home to you but most likely causes a lot of other people to gasp for fresh air.

But what we *see* can be the most important of all. Patients just released from intensive care left the hospital sooner when the picture they saw each day in their room was a beautiful landscape or children playing; they remained hospitalized longer when staring at a vague picture of a tree or at impersonal medical equipment, and longest of all when given an abstract painting to look at daily.

All this strongly suggests that the images created in our consciousness, whether through sight, sound, or smell, play a powerful role in defining our experience of an environment and thus how we behave within it. We create these impressions in the early stages of experiencing an environment, and they remain a nearly indelible part of it even as changes occur and we process new information. First impressions account for more than 50 percent of the entire experience of place.

The exercise that follows can be used in two ways. First, take the test yourself, imagining that you are visiting *you* for the first time. Don't think—just try to feel your responses. Then, give the worksheet to four or five friends or relatives without telling them about it first. Just hand it to them one day when they visit, and ask them to play along for a few minutes as a way to support you. There is no right or wrong, so they can't make any mistakes; although some friends may try to make "safer" responses than others. Encourage them to be completely honest in their evaluations. Then, compare what your friends or family say with what you experience.

FIRST IMPRESSIONS WORKSHEET

Evaluate only what is asked of you. Circle one of the possible responses, or write another response in the space provided.

Remember: Impressions are feelings, not thoughts.

1. What is the first thing you saw when you arrived?

2. If you didn't know who lived here, what would your impressions on the way to the front door tell you?

3. What is the first aroma you notice in the house?

Floral   Musty   Wet   Doggy   Incense   Books
Shoes   Cleanser   Food   Perfume   Wood   Seaside
Meat

4. What patterns did you notice in the entryway?

Checkerboard   Dots   *X*'s   Curved Lines   Stars
Floral Prints   Spirals   Straight Lines   Diamonds

5. What did you hear when you arrived?

Television   Kids   Dog   Music   Electrical Humming
People Talking   Aquarium   Traffic   Heat/AC Vents

6. What did you notice here that needs fixing?

Broken Doorbell   Light Bulb Out   Broken Step
Torn Carpet   Cracked Glass (Window)   Exposed
Wires   Door That Sticks   Water Damage on Wall
Loose Fixture

7. Overall, what is your impression of me, based only on what you have seen so far, responding as if this is the first time you have come here and the relationship with me is completely new?

Warm   Cool   Distant   Serious   Professional
Intimate   Rich   Confused   Busy   Intense   Sexy
Spaced Out   Creative   Plain   Radical   Powerful
Elegant   Artistic   Frigid   Depressed   Healthy
Lonely   Tired   Open-Minded   Cheap   Conservative
Happy   Cold   Worldly   Cautious   Innovative

8. What did you experience in the environment that caused you to circle one of the responses above?

Your Neighborhood

In some orthodox religious cultures, an intentional effort is made to conceal the beauty and ambiance of what is inside the house by making the outside look run-down, poor, and uninviting. This way of creating contrast is thought to keep the neighbors from being envious and prospective burglars uninterested.

In most communities, however, the outside accurately reflects the inside. A driveway and front porch littered with children's toys is quite likely to look like the living spaces inside. A manicured lawn and garden will most often match the orderliness of the kitchen. When considering a neighborhood, therefore, it is useful to take a close look at the houses nearby, for more can be seen than you might think at first. Healthy people and happy families usually care about the way their community looks and will make an effort to keep their homes in good shape. Take a look at your community on your next day off, and see who is out there improving or diminishing your property values! If you are considering a move into a new neighborhood, take a leisurely walk around the block and look *behind* some of those neighbor's houses. Spend some time in the local stores—buy a newspaper or loaf of bread at the corner market and stop by the local convenience store. These may become *your* local haunts and the people who manage them your daily contacts. How does this neighborhood feel? What impression do you have of the other customers? This short excursion can introduce you to the energy of the neighborhood better than any brochure from the local business council; it will be *your* impression, not theirs.

Arriving at Your Home

Modern building codes now dictate that the width of entryways take into consideration the possible need for an emergency exit. As a result, your front door is probably the widest door in your house. Unless you choose to be highly reclusive, the front door should be as wide as possible, inviting the world into your home. The entry should open to a clear path with no intrusion from nearby roads or buildings. Ideally, power lines should not be visible from the front door. The sill or step should be solid and stable. The door itself is best when slightly elevated. If there are many steps, they should be wider at the bottom and narrower at the top.

The hinges, hardware, and door frame should be in good working order, ensuring that the door does not stick in hot or humid weather and that the hinges don't creak. Houses where doors stick have occupants with many frustrations. Where shaky entry stones or creaky hinges rule, those who dwell therein become nervous and insecure.

If the doorplate, knocker, or handle is of a metal like brass that could be polished, make sure it is well cared for. Doors with rusty fixtures usually lead to homes full of timeworn occupants. Check to see if the entryway is well lit at night, if possible, and that light fixtures are kept clean and free of spider webs, dead insects, leaves, or other debris. When choosing a color for the front hall, select one that is slightly darker than the rest of the house; it should, however, be well lit. Dark entryways or dirty light fixtures create confusion, fatigue, and apprehension when entering.

If your entryway is shared, as in a duplex or apartment, make an effort on behalf of the other tenants to make that part of the first impression the best it can be. Welcome mats made of strong fibers, for example, can be a pleasant and economical way to limit the dirt tracked into the building—even if they need to be regularly cleaned or replaced.

Planters or flower boxes outside the front door can very often be a beautiful enhancement; however, nothing looks as bad outside your front door as a dead plant or a huge planter full of dried leaves and cigarette butts. Make sure what *is* there is living and healthy. If a walkway leads up to the door, keep it cleared of seasonal debris like snow, dried leaves, and grass clippings. Prickly bushes, like rose and hawthorn, need to be trimmed back and planted far enough away from the path so as not to in any way obtrude on those who pass either in sight or mind. Brushing up against a bush of thorns— even if only in the mind—makes one recoil and wince in discomfort. When planning borders along narrow pathways, choose rounded-leaf plants like ivy, other ground covers, or small flowers.

Any trees directly in front of the door should be at least twenty to twenty-five feet from the house. If the tree is very small, it may be somewhat closer; if it is immense, it may need to be even farther away so that energy flowing into the house is not inhibited or blocked. A tree that blocks sight of the front door from the street will block the sight of the street from the front door too. This placement creates an excess of Earth energy for the occupants, causing their health to deteriorate; the chapter on health later in the book elucidates issues like this in greater depth. The sight of evergreens near the entrance, on the other hand, will add to the health and well-being of the occupants, provided the trees do not block the entry. Dead trees, or those that are badly damaged by the elements or disease, should be removed.

If the house is surrounded by a wall or fence, it should not be too close to the structure. A constant feeling of being trapped or fenced in can develop if there is too little space between the house and a border.

Pets and Other Creatures, Real and Imagined

Part of the energy of the neighborhood can be easily diagnosed by observing the animals found there. If your neighbors' bird feeders attract only black crows, or the local laundry seems to be overflowing with stray cats, this may not be a healthy community. Take a long look at the kinds of animals, insects (butterflies or mosquitoes?), pets, and other creatures around your house. There is not much disagreement about what is more desirable—a hummingbird in your backyard or a skunk in your garbage. And though you may have little choice, at least you can become more conscious of what *is* there and make adjustments later on to improve the energy in your life by using feng shui outside and around your house.

Your Inner Voice

Finally, if you want to change the first impression your home creates, do so from the direction of your inner voice—not from what you think is correct, but rather from what you *feel* is right. No one says you have to have a wide door. It is simply a matter of understanding what impression choosing to have a narrow door may create— it may be exactly what you want.

And if there is very little opportunity for you to change the outside environment you already have, then so be it! Go ahead and complete the First Impressions Worksheet and move on. The key to beginning to master feng shui is learning to see the big picture.

Chapter 7

From the Outside Looking In

Where the telescope ends, the microscope begins.
Which of the two has the grander view?

VICTOR HUGO

Having completed the worksheets in the previous chapters, it is now time to take a look at how your house can be seen as an expression of your life and how your life is revealed in the spaces where you live and work.

Placing the Bagua

When Fu Hsi sat by the river and observed the tortoise, he set into motion the beginning of a profound way of seeing the world. King Wen and the Duke of Chou brought into view the importance of human consciousness, and with it set down the pattern of spatial arrangement called the bagua.

In reality the same arrangement as the Later Heaven sequence of the *I Ching*, the bagua is like an imaginary grid or map we use to name and relate every area on the horizon. Beginning with our plot, drawn from the point of entry, continuing with the house, each floor and room, each desktop and horizontal surface, the bagua can even be superimposed on your face and your palm as another way to understand your life and destiny.

The method used to orient the bagua in Intuitive Feng Shui is known as the Three-Door Gate of Chi, derived from the magic square of the *I Ching*. In order to accurately apply this method, it is essential to understand clearly which door is to be considered the Front Door. The Front Door is the main entrance, the "gate" through which energy enters your house. It will be the door used almost always by you and your visitors. If this happens to be your back door, and the door on the front of your house hasn't been opened for years, then your back door should be considered your Front Door.

You need to consider this distinction carefully. It is not necessary to use your front door in order to orient the bagua correctly if it is really "out of service." It is important to eliminate it if boxes or furniture block it or if the outside is closed off, forbidding entry. Such a door, essentially never used, is not the "Gate of Chi." If, however, the front door of your house is used very little because you find it more convenient to enter through the kitchen or from the driveway but visitors do sometimes come to the front of your house and enter through this door, then your front door *is* your Front Door. If in doubt, assume that the door architecturally designed to be your main entrance is the Front Door. This, then, will become the starting point for you in understanding how to place your plot and house, like an overlay on the fixed pattern of the bagua.

Even Shapes

In a house that is symmetrical, and basically a regular shape, the application of the bagua is malleable; that is, its shape can be squeezed or stretched *as long as each area remains proportionally the same as in the original*. Considering the shapes in the illustrations, it is easy to see how the bagua can be applied to a narrow house, like a Victorian row

Front Door

Front Door

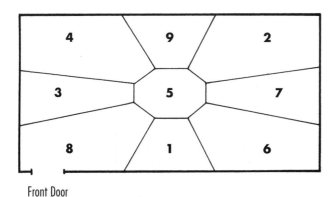

Front Door

Malleable Baguas

house; a long, wide California ranch; a simple square or rectangular house; or virtually any shape of apartment or condominium unit.

The only rule in the Three-Door Gate of Chi method is to place the Front Door at the bottom of the page, facing down. In this way, the Front Door in a symmetrical house will always align directly with 8, 1, or 6. The following examples cover many different possibilities.

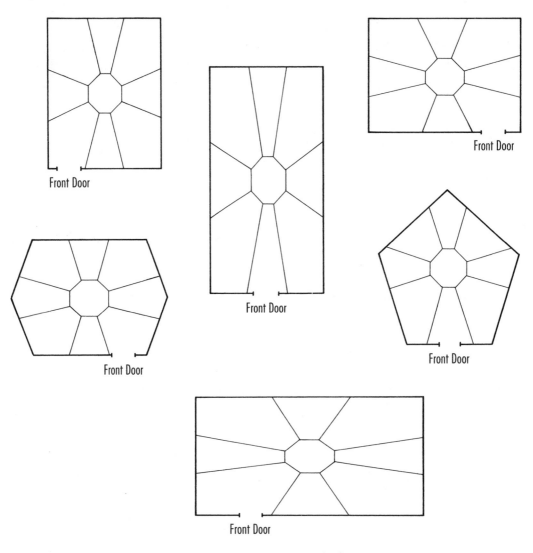

Front Door

Front Door

Front Door

Front Door

Front Door

Front Door

Symmetrical Shapes

Odd Shapes

When the space is not symmetrical, and there is a missing corner or long extension, the bagua can still be applied, even though the door may actually enter another number. To align the bagua, place the Front Door at the bottom of the page and lay it over the magic square. The examples in the following illustrations show how odd-shaped houses can be aligned.

Odd-shaped houses

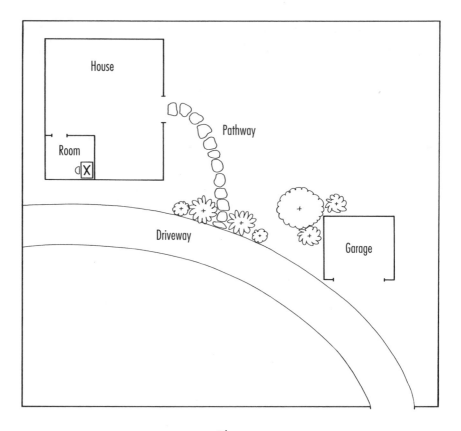

Plot

Every door we pass through creates another bagua. Our plot has an entryway (the drive or path), so there is a bagua for this; the house on the plot has an entry (the Front Door), so there is a bagua for the house; the living room has a Front Door, so it too has a bagua; and your desk in the living room has a Front Door (where you pull in your chair—where you enter your work area) so here too is a bagua. Although each doorway may enter on another plane, as in the next example, each doorway and every area will have a place in a properly aligned bagua. This has tremendous significance, because each area of the bagua symbolizes an important part of our lives.

When we begin to correlate each layering, consecutive bagua of the house, room, and desktop, we can see that certain areas of the house carry a more intense charge of one type of energy. The small *X* on the desk in the previous illustration falls in the *4* area of every bagua. This area is directly related to Fortunate Blessings, sometimes referred to in classical texts as Wealth. When a powerful area like this is located in your house or office, it is possible to put some magic into your practice of Intuitive Feng Shui.

Case History

The Problem: Dr. G. had been losing vast amounts of money in the stock market for nearly a year. Some income-producing property he owned had also begun to falter as tenants moved out in protest over the noise caused by construction taking place at a nearby site. Finally, a malpractice suit filed against him was making his financial woes nearly catastrophic.

The Solution: After attending a weekend seminar on Intuitive Feng Shui, Dr. G. learned how to locate the point in his house and office that related most to his difficulty with money. Not surprisingly, there were piles of bills on his desk in the area of Fortunate Blessing and minor disarray in this area in other locations at home. After clearing the specified areas, he placed a particular enhancement in each to change the energy.

The Result: Five days after he completed the solution, the malpractice suit was dropped. Two days later, the developers of the property near his own where tenants were complaining and moving out approached him. The developers offered him a huge sum of money to sell his building so that they could expand their project. And a company in which he had just purchased a large block of stock was unexpectedly taken over by a larger company, producing a windfall for investors.

Chapter 8

Home Shui Home

There's no place like home, there's no place like home,
there's no place like home, there's no place like home...
Dorothy, *The Wizard of Oz*

The Bagua in the House

The most important bagua to understand is that of the area where you spend most of your time. In general, this means your house; in particular, the bedroom or the office. If you sleep only five hours a night but work ten hours a day, use this chapter to understand how to change your office and read Chapter 15. Remember, the more you begin to see how the bagua can be applied in every space, the more control you can begin to have over your life.

If you share a hallway with another tenant in your house, the bagua is sited where your own Front Door begins and does not include the shared hallway. If you live in a second-floor apartment, or on the top floor of a house where others live on the lower floors, the bagua begins where the top step meets your "ground level," which, even if no physical door is present, is your Front Door.

When trying to distinguish where the bagua for each room begins—within your house—it is not necessary to have an actual doorway. In a home or office with an open floor plan, sometimes only a planter box or a counter with an opening divides living or work areas. In some cases, spaces are divided by a change in flooring materials: the kitchen is tile or bare wood and the dining area covered by a carpet. This arrangement creates a line of demarcation that becomes the Front Door for purposes of placing a new bagua over each area or "room."

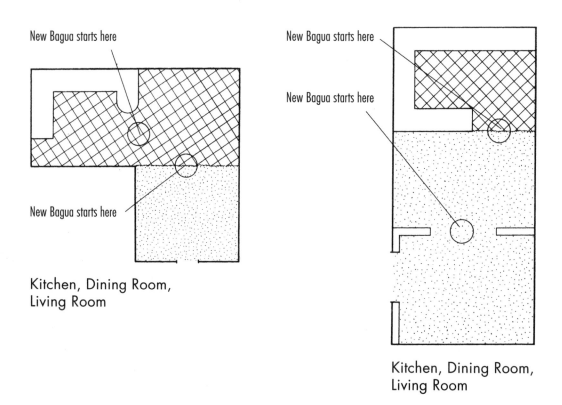

New Bagua starts here

New Bagua starts here

New Bagua starts here

New Bagua starts here

New Bagua starts here

Kitchen, Dining Room,
Living Room

Kitchen, Dining Room,
Living Room

Each floor has a bagua, but it is unnecessary to connect the baguas between floors. The bagua for a new floor begins where the top step meets floor level. Each room on every floor will fall into one of the areas of the bagua, and each room has its own bagua.

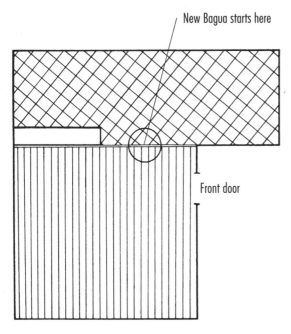

New Bagua starts here

Front door

Kitchen, Dining Room

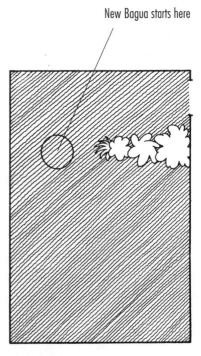

New Bagua starts here

Reception Area,
Office

Front door

New Bagua starts here

Meditation, Alcove,
Sleep Area

Thirty spokes share the wheel's hub;

It is the center hole that makes it useful.

Shape clay into a vessel;

It is the space within that makes it useful.

Cut doors and windows for a room;

It is the holes that make it useful.

Therefore profit comes from what is there;

Usefulness from what is not there.

—LAO TSU

Something Lost

After you align the bagua with a floor plan to locate the many possible associations, it will be clear that some area of your life as represented in the bagua may actually be missing, because the shape of the house or room is not usually a perfect square or rectangle. For example, on the floor plans in the next illustration, part or all of one "house" of the nine that occur in every plan is notched out of the whole. The area that is missing is called negative space. Rather than suggesting that something is bad or undesirable, *negative* implies only that the space is missing, as defined by an invisible boundary created from the remaining structure.

Every structure's energy or vibrational field is symmetrical, even though the visible, material form may be asymmetrical. Each area appearing in negative space is defined by what is there. Fortunately, most people will have some negative space in their floor plan. Life would be pretty boring if everything were in perfect harmony, as King Wen and the Duke of Chou observed 3,200 years ago. Negative space allows *possibility*.

In Intuitive Feng Shui, possibility is unlimited, so do not consider it a problem if you discover more than one house of the bagua missing in your home or office. Most imbalances that you discover can lead to opportunities for bringing positive changes to your environment and to your life.

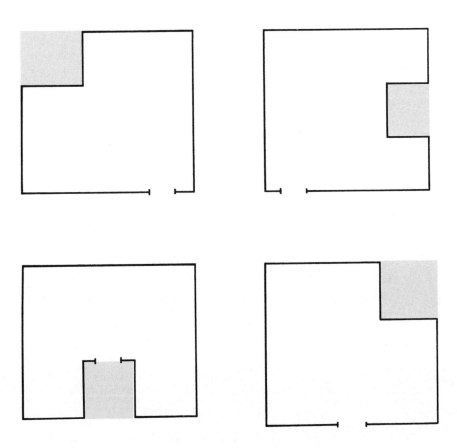

Floor Plans Showing
Negative Space

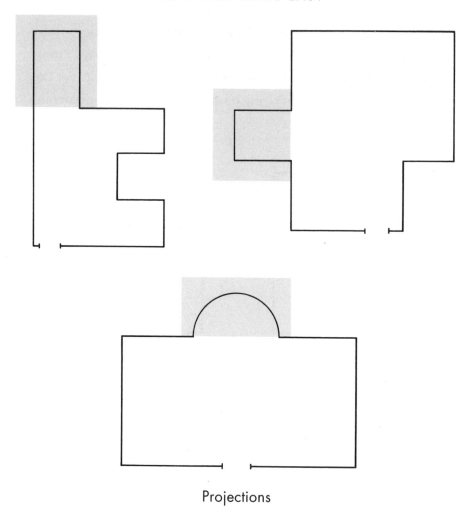

Projections

Something Gained

In contrast to negative space, there are many designs in which an extension from the room creates an alcove, seating area, or larger space that extends out from the whole. This area is called a projection, and it cannot occur parallel to a negative space. An asymmetrical floor plan may create both projections and negative spaces, but they will not fall next to each other.

92

If an area of a room extends away from the symmetrical whole and uses up more than 50 percent of the width of the space, it creates a negative space and is no longer considered a projection; however, if it is less than 50 percent, no negative space is created, and the interior area *is* a projection. The floor plans in the illustration show some commonly occurring examples of projections.

Placing the Bagua on Negative Space and Projections

CASE HISTORY

The Problem: Ms. S. was a wonderfully creative, successful artist with many girlfriends, a good relationship with her family, and a beautiful apartment. She had been practicing meditation for eight years and felt very fulfilled and centered in her life, although she continued to search for a mate. Despite encounters with many available men, Ms. S. never seemed to be able to attract Mr. Right. After a few seminars on relationships, years of productive therapy, and countless blind dates with everyone else's perfect man, she was still single.

The Solution: Ms. S. heard about feng shui from a friend who attended a workshop where the teacher drew a floor plan showing an apartment with the negative space in Earth, the house of Relationships. It was exactly like Ms. S's home! Her friend told her how to make adjustments to cure the problem, which included placing a mirror on the wall where the Earth corner was missing, and she went home to carry them out.

The Result: In the week that followed, Ms. S. met a man

at an art gallery where her work was displayed. He asked her out, they began to see each other over the next few months, and he proposed marriage six months later. She is now, quite blissfully, Mrs. N.

Fixed Placements

There are some placements that are so difficult to cure, even with feng shui, that they should be avoided. An obvious example of poor design would be a toilet that opens directly into a kitchen, causing a mixing of two distinctly different energies. Other fixed placements to avoid for toilets are in the area of Wind (where Fortunate Blessings will be flushed away), directly opposite the Front Door (where occupants and visitors will experience the toilet as their first impression), and in the center of the house (where the energy of Water and waste could create sickness and mental instability for the occupants).

Another difficult situation is an arrangement of rooms and corridors that cause doors to bang into each other or obstruct or severely limit free passage. Doors opening into a hallway that bang into others from a closet, for example, can cause occupants to argue (their opinions may "clash") and the house to be loud (banging doors). These examples are fixed placements and may be costly, impractical, or physically impossible to remedy, although some approaches mentioned later on in the book may be used to lessen a chronic problem.

Fluid Placements

Where you put your bed, desk, or stove is usually a matter of choice and offers you a number of different options for arranging the space.

Fluid placements can be moved and changed, and some basic principles apply.

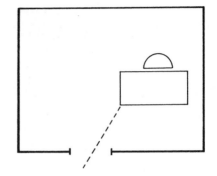

1. *Power and security* come from maintaining a wide view. In any space where you sit or sleep, position furniture to give yourself the biggest view of the room and doorway. The ancient symbol of the Dragon was meant to be behind us, that is, situated for security and backup. Do not place yourself in a way that exposes your blind side, behind you.

2. The doorway is the gate or mouth of energy into the room. Do not position a bed or desk directly opposite the door, but rather slightly off to one side in order to increase the breadth of view and scope of the whole room. As little space as possible should be behind you. In front of you, at an entryway or door, you may choose to place some sort of guardian for protection. These symbols appear in many cultures and include lions or dogs on both sides of a doorway and religious articles mounted on the wall near the door. They are said to protect and "lift" the house to higher energies.

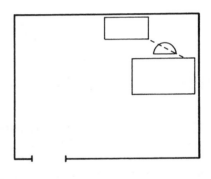

3. Beware of invisible lines of energy that radiate from the right angles of furniture at the 45-degree point. These lines, called

cutting chi, intensify energy focus and cause subliminal discomfort and obstruction. A slight modification in placement can remedy cutting chi, or in some cases the use of plants or soft fabrics in front of the angle may be necessary.

Cutting chi is knifelike energy that emanates from the mass of all 90-degree angles. Because most modern structures are built with T-squares, there are likely to be many such angles in your environment. Those that create cutting chi of the most concern will send a vibrational field out of the mass at 45 degrees into a chair, bed, or dining table where people will feel uncomfortable. If possible, place furniture in a room far away from and out of the line of this energy; if not, you will need to make corrections to disperse or soften this force.

In the illustrations that follow, see if you can see what fluid placements can be changed to improve the room. Look for examples of cutting chi, loss of power or security, and common mistakes that can be easily corrected.

Kitchens and Stoves

Proper placement of the stove in a kitchen has always been considered one of the most important aspects of good feng shui. The kitchen, where food is prepared and life sustained, is the symbolic source of wealth and well being in the home.

A stove placed in an island or freestanding counter is fine, providing that it is not directly opposite a sink and the burners are secured from behind with a short, vertical backsplash. Water and Fire need to be balanced and apart but should not be placed in exact opposition. If a stove is sited in a corner or supported by two walls and allows an open (or partial) view of the door, the cook will feel in greater control of the space, more secure and protected. This placement is also symbolic of increasing the wealth of the occupants. Stoves should not be placed under windows or under skylights. The energy of food preparation will leave the house rather than be absorbed by its occupants.

Placing stoves next to sinks or refrigerators (fire and water, hot and cold) creates conflict and danger. To remedy this placement, common in many homes, a small plant on the counter or hanging in the space in between will allow a smoother flow of energy from water to wood to fire, along the natural cycle of creation as described in the theory of Five Transformations. A photograph or painting of plants or wood will also serve to bring about a greater sense of harmony.

The kitchen itself should be considered the most important room in the house. It is here that we create life through our daily food. The shape of the kitchen, therefore, should be most simple and balanced. The ceiling should be neither cathedral-like nor very low. It must be a comfortable space in which anyone can create harmony, balance, and health through food preparation.

If possible, place the stove so that it faces the east or light (south in the northern hemisphere, north in the southern hemisphere). Other directions are less auspicious but not necessarily disastrous. The best placement for a stove affords the cook with natural light from as many of the four cardinal directions as possible. Eating areas nearby should be calm, clear, and uncluttered with a peaceful feeling emanating from artwork, color selection, or choice of objects.

Bedrooms and Sleeping Areas

Most of us will spend one-third of our lives asleep. Good feng shui in the bedroom means peaceful, restorative energy for rest and rejuvenation. As this room is primarily for sleeping and recovering energy, its colors, artwork, and other objects should convey peace. Televisions, stereos, or entertainment areas are better placed far away from the bed—ideally in a completely different room. The bedroom is best sited at the rear of a house—away from the front door—where we can retreat at the end of a long day to unwind and relax.

The proper placement of the bed depends upon many things, the most important of which is practicality. Ideally, its placement should result in easy access when making the bed and changing linens. The bed should not block closet doors or passage to dressing areas or bathrooms. As in the placement of a desk, the most auspicious location for the bed is opposite the door, diagonally across from the entry in the opposite corner—not necessarily against the wall—allowing for a feeling of space around the bed and a commanding view of the entire room and all who enter.

When a bed must be placed under slanted ceilings or eaves, it is a good idea to minimize the effect of imbalanced air circulation this placement causes. Occupants should install canopies or light material hung from the ceiling that covers the width and length of the whole bed, running parallel to the sleeping surface. Soffits extending from the back wall should not extend more than a few inches, as they can cause an oppressive overhang above the heads of those sleeping below.

Side tables, headboards, and nearby furnishings such as dressers, nightstands, and valets should have slightly rounded edges or be placed in such a way as to eliminate cutting chi. It is best when there is no passageway behind the head of the bed, nor should there be a large window directly behind or above the headboard; there may, however, be a small opening higher up on the wall behind the bed for ventilation and light. Most important, the lasting impression we have as we enter the "dream state" will be a result of what we see as we go to sleep. It is therefore very important that artwork, furnishings, and other accessories visible from our bedside be pleasant and harmonious, conveying a feeling of relaxation, calm, and order. This is another good reason to leave the television out of the bedroom entirely. Like seeing our desks piled with papers or clothes hampers overflowing with dirty laundry, disturbing images on the evening news subtly disrupt and negatively affect our sleeping hours.

Living Areas

In general, the living room is a reflection of our family life. It is the ideal place to display our "treasures" of art, culture, and history. It should be a comfortable, well-lit showplace where we are proud to be seen with family and friends. Seating areas in the living room should create a sense of security for both occupants and guests. Couches and chairs should be placed so that they are protected from behind. A wall, bookcase, or side table with plantings can serve this purpose. Seats that seem to float in the middle of a room, rather than being grouped together with other furnishings, should have side or end tables nearby for stability.

Chapter 9

You Are Where You Live

*Your house is your larger body. It grows in the sun and
sleeps in the stillness of the night; and it is not dreamless.
Does not your house dream? and dreaming, leave the city
for grove or hilltop?*

KAHLIL GIBRAN, *THE PROPHET*

Man's character is the product of his premises.

AYN RAND, *THE FOUNTAINHEAD*

The House Defined

Every area of your house—every *house* of the bagua—carries a different energy and symbolic "charge." After completing the Self-Evaluation Worksheet in Chapter 1, you should have a good grasp of these areas. The purpose of this chapter is to understand what each house means and where to locate these energies in your own home or work environment. If you have completed the exercises on aligning the bagua, it is now time to create the map for your life as it manifests in your home or office. Highlight those areas you wish to enhance, change, or adjust using the cures that you will learn after reading the next chapter.

Symbols of the Bagua

1. WATER

The area of Water is the beginning,
called The Journey.

Stand before it and there is no beginning.
Follow it and there is no end.

LAO TSU

Life proceeds along a path; it is our personal journey. This area of our life is like riding in a boat down a river. The Water area is sometimes called Career, but it is much more than your job. It represents the freedom to do what you want to do—for life to flow effortlessly, with clarity and ease. It is a natural site to include objects containing liquid, such as inks, paint, medicine, or oil, or art that depicts or symbolizes water in some way, including rivers, streams, oceans, fish, whales, and waterfalls.

When this area is missing from the bagua in your home, some occupant of the house may suffer from illness unless it is corrected by placement. If there is a projection in this area, the occupants will usually acquire wealth and have a keen understanding of how to use it.

2. EARTH

The area of Earth corresponds
to Relationships.

I want to be with those who know secret things, or else alone.
I want to be a mirror for your whole body.
RAINER MARIA RILKE

Relationships with others, whether platonic, professional, or passionate, help us to become better integrated with parts of ourselves we cannot so easily see. For some, relationships with clients or customers mean money; for others, relationships are the source of great happiness, resulting in marriage and the beginning of family—for many, the main focus of life. Earth, the Receptive, symbolizes the essence of this area. Earth corresponds to all things that receive, like cushions or pillows (they receive your body), fields and uncultivated land (open areas), and the highest nature of sincere modesty, basic humility and an empty, giving, open heart. To be in a relationship means to be truly receptive as well as naturally giving.

The inner world of relationships is 180 degrees across the bagua, called Contemplation. Our relationships with others are always a result of how we carry them within ourselves. Earth is the area that carries the strongest charge of the Feminine Principle.

When this area is missing from the bagua in a house, women may have trouble living there. Occupants may also have difficulty with issues involving land or agriculture. When it is a projection, the house will be happiest when many women live there, although men may be much less happy in such a house.

3. THUNDER

The area of Thunder is the energy
of our Elders.

If ye don't know the past, then ye will not have a future.
If ye don't know where your people have been, then ye
won't know where your people are going.
FORREST CARTER, *THE EDUCATION OF LITTLE TREE*

Like the thunder that precedes the storm, our elders and ancestors
come before us. Respect and honor for them is a traditional principle all but lost in modern society. This area relates directly to those
who are your superiors, bosses, parents, and elders; some of them are
in your biological family, but included are those above you in your
work environment as well. Associated with energy that moves
upward and outward like a tree, Thunder or Elders is also symbolized by musical instruments (noisemakers), tall plants (upward
growth), sunrise, and other aspects of this energy depicted in art or
objects. This area is 180 degrees opposite the house that rules children and offspring, the Lake.

When there is an indentation or a missing part of the house in Thunder, occupants are liable to feel a loss of energy and lack of endurance and vitality. Children born in these houses may leave home at a very early age. When there is a projection in this area, the energy created in the house will lead to greater success in life for the occupants.

4. WIND

The area of Wind is the place
of Fortunate Blessings.

Should you shield the canyons from the windstorms,
you would never see the beauty of their carvings.

ELISABETH KÜBLER-ROSS

Just to be is a blessing. Just to live is holy.

RABBI ABRAHAM HESCHEL

Most people associate good luck with winning the lottery, picking
the right horse at the racetrack, or receiving an unexpected gift,
such as an inheritance or the prize at a raffle. At feng shui seminars, many participants are eager to identify this area of their home
and to activate it to increase their income. The area of Wind, though
often associated with wealth, is more accurately the area where we
experience blessing in our lives—even in the midst of great difficulty—and remember just how blessed we truly are.

Not just being on the receiving end of dollars, to be in Fortunate
Blessings means to have a very real perception and experience of

good luck in many areas of life, to be blessed by good omens, prosperity, harmony, and even health. Acknowledgment by a coworker or employer, gratitude expressed by a sibling, a promotion at work, or honors received through a trade association are all signs of Wind in harmony.

The symbol of penetration, like wind blowing through a screen, and the lighter aspects of the tree nature of palms or willows are more closely related to this area and can be enhanced through art and other symbolic objects. Directly opposite Wind, 180 degrees across the bagua, is Heaven, which rules philanthropy. Of course, the more blessings we receive, the more we can give away.

When Wind is absent in a house, the occupants will have more frequent accidents and experience "bad luck." They will frequently have difficulty with business affairs, documents, legal contracts, and taxes. If this area is a projection, occupants are often very successful in business and generally enjoy "good luck" and fortune.

5. THE TAI CHI

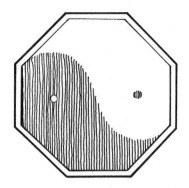

The center, called the Tai Chi,
symbolizes all complementary
antagonisms and Unity.

Every man is in touch with everything else, not through his hands,
though, but through a bunch of long fibers that shoot out from the
center of his abdomen. These fibers join a man to his surroundings;
they keep his balance; they give him stability.

CARLOS CASTANEDA,
FURTHER CONVERSATIONS WITH DON JUAN

The vital center of the body, called the *hara,* is the deep, rooted space
from which life's energy, or chi, emanates. Like the gravitational
midpoint of our anatomy, the Tai Chi in a room or house is the place
of profound Unity. Here, in the center of the home, many traditional cultures and families would bring complementary aspects
from the outside, like a small courtyard with a garden or atrium.
Most of all, Unity must be uncluttered, clean, and orderly. More a
point of reference than an actual space with certain dimensions,
Unity contains aspects of all eight trigrams and may be the most

important part of your home or office if your main concern is health. To be truly healthy is to unite the best aspects of all eight houses in the bagua—good relationships with friends and family, a satisfying career, feelings of being blessed, and so on. The Tai Chi contains "everything" and "nothing."

When this area is missing, then the outside is inside—there is a courtyard or garden in the center! This is a wonderful design used by many traditional cultures, but take note: placing water in this area is wise only if the water remains fresh, active, and moving. When stagnant water resides here, the occupants of a home can become ill, their nervous systems frayed, and families may experience grave hardships. The overall dimension of an outdoor or garden area in the Tai Chi should be less than one-third of the total usable indoor space.

6. HEAVEN

The area of Heaven is the door open
to Helpful Friends.

*Follow the way of heaven, reflect on the principle
behind human affairs.*
HAN FEI TZU, THIRD CENTURY BCE

Do as you would be done by.
FOURTEENTH-CENTURY ENGLISH PROVERB

The way of nature is the way of Heaven. Gifts from above, as manifest on the earth, occur in the form of support, guidance, and love from close friends. This area, Helpful Friends, is the door through which volunteers, supportive staff, good neighbors, and "angels" of the figurative and real variety may enter your life. It is also the area through which you, as a helpful friend in other people's lives, serve by giving away your talents, time, and energy unconditionally. The essence of this area of our house is philanthropy—not through donations of cash to a charity or tithing to a church, but through our own selfless acts of giving away what is most important to us without expecting anything in return. Semiprecious gemstones, diamonds, and lead crystal objects symbolize this energy. Heaven also embodies the strongest charge of the masculine principle, energetically opposite the image of Earth's feminine charge.

When this area of the bagua is missing from the house, a man will have difficulty with his employers. He may also suffer from illness and lack vitality. When this area is projected, occupants will more naturally be able to develop a concern for their fellow human beings and act in ways that support people in the society who have less material wealth.

7. LAKE

The area of the Lake is related
to our Creativity.

"_____"

[BE CREATIVE! FILL IN THE BLANK SPACE PROVIDED ABOVE.]

All that we create—our children, projects, stories, and masterpieces of the art world—come from the energy of the Lake. Often called Offspring, this area of our house brings a youthful joy and imagination into being. Here, we develop plans for a new store, invent a better mousetrap, give birth to a poem or song, and plant the seeds of new life. Creativity lives in all of us, large and small, young and old. With it, life is magical; without it, life is over. This area of our house also symbolizes all the related aspects of the sensory organs: taste, touch, smell, sight, and hearing. In particular, fragrant blossoms, glistening ponds, delicious desserts, and melodious music enhance the essence of the Lake, as do images of these aspects presented in art and objects. This area is also associated with twilight, immediately before sunset.

When this part of the bagua is missing in the house, occupants will have difficulty saving money for their own enjoyment. They will tend to spend it or give it away foolishly. When there is a projection in this area, occupants will be sociable, happy, and well fed, although they may often be the brunt of ridiculous gossip!

8. MOUNTAIN

The Mountain is the area of quiet
Contemplation.

*To be conscious that you are ignorant
is a great step to knowledge.*

BENJAMIN DISRAELI

Ancient sages spent hours in quiet contemplation, often amid the clear air and quiet solitude of a mountain cave. Following hours of study or meditation, the ancients would face their worldly ignorance and deepen their knowledge of self. This area in our house, also referred to as Inner Knowledge, does not come from what you know, but instead is charged by what you *don't* know. A college diploma, graduate degree, or honors award in the Department of Intellect may be an important measure to some, but thousands of the world's greatest teachers, philosophers, masters, artists, and mentors drew their wisdom from within—and had no certification or credit from a university. Inner knowledge depends on self-reflection or introspection, often carried out late at night or in the early hours of the morning. The mountain is symbolized by containers (like caves), churches, solitary items, empty boxes or vessels, and the stillness of nature in the wintertime.

When this area of the bagua is missing in the house or is indented, a couple living there may find it difficult to conceive a child. A single woman may have difficulty with her reproductive organs. A projection in this area also leads to difficulty for the inhabitants. Family arguments and tension will abound as each person becomes more and more selfish. This is the one house of the bagua that should ideally have neither a projection nor an indentation.

9. FIRE

The area of Fire, completing the
bagua, is Illumination.

Before enlightenment, carry water, chop wood.
After enlightenment, carry water, chop wood.
ANONYMOUS

Being charged by Fire means manifesting an energy of clarity. At
the end of the cycle, as at the end of life, we finally see that light
shines from within. When we are in the spotlight or the public eye,
this area might be called Fame. But it is clear that public recognition or worldwide exposure can still leave a superstar in the dark.
This area of the house corresponds not to being in the spotlight but
rather to illumination from within and the ability to illuminate or
enlighten others. It is symbolized by the active, pulsating energy of
summer and is enhanced by objects that illuminate the soul, like
great works of literature, Old Master paintings, or deeply moving
music or poetry. Fire is 180 degrees opposite the house of Water,
reminding us that we are constantly in relationship to our path and
must always be doing what we want to do. Many people, after

achieving fame and material success, are ruled by the demands placed upon them as a result of their newfound popularity. This may take them away from their path, The Journey, the house of Water—always in relationship with Fire. Many famous artists and political figures leave behind the glitter and notoriety to pursue a dream more true to their inner nature. Enlightened masters abandon desire. The mastery of Fire distinguishes human beings from all the other animals.

When this part of the bagua is missing from the house, occupants will be overly concerned about other people's opinions and find it difficult to develop self-confidence. When it is a projection, the energy that is created will often cause people to become well-known in society or to achieve a state of self-realization through daily life.

Everything Is Connected

The nature of the bagua, as Fu Hsi envisioned it, was actually quite an extraordinary concept: everything in our world—every material object, emotion, color, occupation, spiritual quality, season, and so on—could be considered a part of one area of the bagua. Nothing is left out of the whole. Everything in our lives will fall under the influence of the energy of one of the nine areas, or houses, of the bagua in our home.

Imagine that you are working in the mailroom of the local newspaper. Although you aren't getting rich, working for a large company has certain benefits and does pay the bills. But as a hobby, you have recently taken up fine woodworking. You buy yourself a set of tools and read the trade magazines devoted to cabinetmaking. You create a few small things and give them away as presents to your friends. You soon realize that you might even make some good money by selling your work.

So, as an amateur carpenter, you decide to try your hand at building a freestanding wardrobe (armoire) and then offer it for sale in your local newspaper.

At the start of a project like this, your energy is rising like Thunder, associated with "birth" and new ideas. Envisioning, designing, and creating the piece would be ruled by the Lake, the house of Creativity; selling it would be ruled by Wind, the house of Fortunate Blessings, because a sale would result in money coming toward you.

After the first sale, you might very well become excited by the prospect of leaving your office job and earning a living designing wardrobes. This new direction in life would be ruled by Water, because it changes the course of The Journey. Because wardrobes are really big boxes, the actual pieces you create are strongly influenced by the Mountain, because physical forms like boxes relate to Contemplation.

As you get started, you find it is necessary to apprentice to a master craftsman. He or she would be ruled by Thunder, as this house also contains the energy of Elders. While working under the master's guidance, you meet another person who has been designing kitchen cupboards. This person has just started out in furniture making, and the two of you talk about beginning to work together, setting up a business making custom pieces. Earth, the area of your home covering Relationships, influences the association with your new partner. You discuss a few names for the new business and decide that it will be called Clearlight Furniture Design Company. A name like that would be closely related to Fire, the nature of Illumination.

The two of you need a lot of guidance and support to successfully market your products, but you don't have much money to go out and hire a sales representative or business manager. You know a few friends whose advice could really help you get started. Heaven, the area of Helpful Friends, will influence them.

These distinctions go on and on, connecting almost everything you do with all the other parts, and relating the whole to the bagua. Take a moment to reflect on what you are doing now and where certain aspects of this work fall in the bagua. Are there any trouble spots? Roadblocks? Difficulties? Each area of your life will correspond to one of the houses of the bagua.

CASE HISTORY

The Problem: Lucy wrote a great biography about a famous person from the twenties. Everyone who read it thought it was wonderful, but she couldn't find a publisher. She sent her manuscript out to many agents and editors but got back the same rejection letters and polite refusals.

The Solution: After talking with a relative who had studied Intuitive Feng Shui, Lucy learned how to locate the point in her house and office that related most to her difficulty with not getting her book published. It was the house of Water; not surprisingly, there was a huge mess in her front hallway, the area of The Journey, where her new path would be influenced. After clearing out boxes of old junk, she tore up the carpet, painted the walls a light shade of green, and placed bright paintings and colorful hangings on the wall to stimulate and change the energy.

The Result: Before the end of that week, she received a letter from a publisher agreeing to take her book. After she made additional changes, her agent called her to report that a famous actress and director wanted to buy the rights to the book for a possible project. She signed an option worth much more than she'd ever make on the sale of the book alone!

The houses of the bagua, like every aspect of your life, are intimately joined. As with holistic medicine, you really cannot approach the part and expect to cure the whole person. Looking at your life and living spaces, you will soon see the connection between each room, like parts of the body, and with each aspect of your life, like parts of your soul. Take a moment to look at the bagua again to see how everything is connected.

Chapter 10

Placing Changes

All changes, as well as so-called balance or equilibrium, are
produced and given life by the intersecting of opposites.
GEORGES OHSAWA

What Is a Cure?

Rearranging furniture in a room almost always brings a bit of fresh
air into the life of the occupants. Hang a new picture, cover a chair
with new fabric, or paint a wall and you're likely to improve the
aesthetic. Using the principles of balance and harmony, the corner-
stones of Intuitive Feng Shui, the changes you make in your environment will make a huge difference in your life.

In the practice of medicine, meditation, or mediation, the goal is
to achieve stability near the middle—the act of bringing the focus
of energy closer to the center point. Whether it is a simple cure for
hiccups or the resolution of a long-standing conflict in society, most
"cures" are a coalescing of opposites to create a unified whole. Noise-
cancelling headphones were invented using this principle, achieving
results by producing sounds that offset the unwanted ones.

Even when dealing with the invisible world of vibrations, scientists know through studies that everything we cannot see or touch
can ultimately be categorized as a series of wavelengths created by
the material world. The angstroms of the color spectrum, the frequency of sounds, and the density of materials are all measurable
energies.

The association of feng shui with myth and superstition was born out of a lack of appreciation by modern people for the qualities that exist in the invisible world. For the eye untrained in assessing these energies, feng shui cures appear to be merely remnants of an unenlightened age; however, upon closer examination of most of the basic remedies used in classical feng shui, it is quite apparent that the ancient practitioner was using a principle of balance or harmony in every situation. A striking example of this practice can be seen in the story "The Little Mountain House."

In an age long ago there lived a family in a little mountain house. The daughter, who slept in a small room at the front of this house overlooking the valley, complained of feelings of insecurity and light-headedness. She often thought of her path in life as being unstable and precarious.

The son, who lived in the room on the opposite side at the back, had very different feelings. Despite the love and support of his parents, he often complained of feeling confused, blocked, and depressed. Rigidity and oppression ruled his unhappy life, and few could understand why he was so miserable.

His wise parents decided to seek the advice of the feng shui master who lived in a small village nearby. When the master arrived at the house and observed the surrounding landscape, he quickly saw why the children were experiencing life in such different ways. Using the Unifying Principle, he quickly resolved the problem.

He made some simple recommendations for chi adjustment that would change how the occupants experienced the energies of the house. Behind the house, outside the boy's window, he planted bamboo. This would grow quickly and provide all of the energies opposite to the energies of the mountain. Bamboo is hollow and flexible (the mountain, solid and rigid); it sprouts quickly upward with fresh, vegetable energy (the mountain was very old mineral energy); and the plant was light and pleasant (the mountain, dark, heavy, and ominous). In front of the house, he secured long timbers and heavy stones, creating stability and horizontal energy (the cliff, a precarious drop downward, gave an insecure sensation of the vertical).

Shortly after his visit, when the "cures" were all in place, the parents began to notice subtle but distinct changes in the behavior of their children. And by the start of the next cycle of the moon, both children had become happier than they had ever been.

Where Do Cures Come From?

Most observers of the feng shui art of placement, whether they are historians, architects, or interested homeowners, assume that the cures spoken of for ages have been handed down from some wise man on a mountaintop. When feng shui is viewed as a collection of superstitious remedies, it seems to depend upon connection to some body of secret teachings.

In reality, all the adjustments used by the masters applied the Unifying Principle of harmonizing opposites. Let's imagine that the master the family consulted arrived on the scene with nothing more than a pad and pencil. Sitting behind the house, he began to make a list of the qualities of the mountain's energy that would affect the occupants living at the back. The list might have been something like this:

Down	Mineral
Hard	Still
Dark	Rigid
Old	Solid

In order for his recommendations to work, he knew that any cure he suggested must not add these elements. At first, he thought of a small fountain, because it had the elements of Water within it that were missing. But this did not seem to be enough. Then he envisioned some flowers around the fountain but realized that this too, fell short of the cure needed to balance this huge force. Then he thought of planting a few large trees, which would add other elements that the fountain and flowers alone lacked. But this, he knew, would take time.

Sitting behind the house, the master made another list of all the opposites to what he'd written down before:

Up	Vegetable
Soft	Flowing
Light	Flexible
Young	Hollow

He would have to advise placement of something containing these elements in order to bring harmony to the site. It was then, after using the principle of complementary opposites known as the Unifying Principle, that he saw the perfect solution: plant bamboo behind the house. Bamboo is a rapidly growing, hollow, flexible, fresh plant that sprouts upward with new life in a very short time. The bamboo planted between the house and the mountain conveyed all its energies to those who looked outside the window, essentially neutralizing the effects of the mountain, which had caused the boy to experience life as so difficult. There was nothing unusual about the recommendation at all—it was simply the application of a timeless principle used in all other aspects of life that has worked for thousands of years.

Applying the same principle in front of the house, the master recommended the installation of well-rooted plants in large, solid vases; wide steps secured firmly to the hillside; flowerboxes outside the windows overlooking the hillside planted with flora that would reveal its strong root structure; and other objects that would convey a feeling of stability, safety, and grounding missing from the view out the daughter's window. These cures helped her to gain an experience of the horizontal energy that was missing.

Understanding the Unifying Principle

Life is a series of never-ending changes. Seen through the magic spectacles of the Unifying Principle, energy can be seen as moving in and out, up and down, fast and slow, hot and cold, and so on.

Energy moving in a centripetal way contracts inward, becoming smaller and denser. As it does, molecules begin to vibrate faster, creating friction and heat. As the temperature rises, molecules expand and, as the principle predicts, begin the opposite kind of movement, centrifugal. The energy moves outward and becomes larger and less dense as the molecules begin to move more slowly. As energy slows, the temperature lowers until the whole begins to contract again.

This universal principle of energy has been observed as a complete cycle of change and is applicable in such seemingly diverse and unrelated fields as biology, physics, economics, and history. Using these principles to understand the imbalances present in the environment is the heart of Intuitive Feng Shui. It is easy to see that cures do not originate from some mystical teachings of a forgotten time but are a result of sound judgment and clarity.

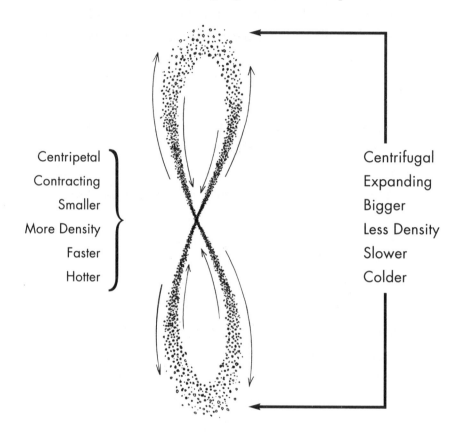

Centripetal
Contracting
Smaller
More Density
Faster
Hotter

Centrifugal
Expanding
Bigger
Less Density
Slower
Colder

The Role of Intuition

There is no logical way to the discovery of these elemental laws. There is only the way of intuition, which is helped by a feeling for the order lying behind appearance.

ALBERT EINSTEIN

Our intuition is an inborn, original ability that develops (like a muscle) with repeated use. We are all born with an instinctual "knowing" based not on learned information or data but on clarity. Everyone has had the experience of "having a hunch," when we find ourselves saying, "I knew that was going to happen!" The challenge is not so much to recognize it in hindsight but to follow it as a source of wisdom and guidance when it first appears. Like an internal geomancer's compass, our intuition is like a magnet, guided by the clear, unblocked stream of energy that flows between heaven and earth along our spine. An infinite, universal knowing available to every human being, intuition is attracted to the opposite magnetic poles of iron molecules in our red blood cells. As we clean our blood through proper diet and way of life, our overall condition improves, allowing us to observe energy clearly, with a higher level of judgment.

Using the Unifying Principle in Intuitive Feng Shui, the practitioner gains access to the key issue in every problem. Without it, you are watching the soccer game from behind a goalpost; with it, your seat is at the center of the stadium. It is essential to understand that intuition strengthens as a result of *internal clarity* and has nothing to do with accumulating data.

Putting Feng Shui in Your Life: Clutter and Clearing

Because the internal and external worlds are a reflection of each other, gaining clarity can begin from either environment. Before going on, take some time to clear the spaces you intend to "cure" with feng shui. Eliminate the clutter. The cures detailed in the next section will have a profound effect on your life and destiny. How successful you are in achieving the desired results depends upon two extremely important considerations: *place* and *purpose*.

Whether you are installing cures in your home or your work environment, it is essential to maximize the transforming power of feng shui by first preparing the space. Placing mirrors or hanging crystals in a disorderly or cluttered room can have negative effects. Much like fasting or eating only a light meal the night before surgery, clearing the environment before implementing the cure allows greater positive change to occur.

Place

Remove all clutter from the place where you intend to practice feng shui. If you are a collector by nature, change what could be considered clutter into storage—a very different type of energy. All those bags of clothes that do not fit anymore or are out of style are *clutter.* Winter clothes you are not wearing in the summer are storage. Piles of magazines that you keep around just in case you want to refer to that article from four years ago are *clutter.* An organized collection of back issues of your favorite magazine is storage. Stacks of books and records, shelves full of old CDs you never listen to anymore, and the stacks of photographs that didn't quite turn out are all *clutter* until you organize them neatly. Once you begin to look around, do not be surprised to see how much clutter you have accumulated! A thorough "spring cleaning" of your household is a good first step.

You mean to say, after all we have learned here,
that the first step of feng shui is more housework?
Seminar participant

    The windowsills, walls, and doorways where you might install one of the many cures should be cleared of objects, decals, and other extras. A simple cleaning will also change the energy where the cures will be placed. You may also wish to perform a simple space-clearing ritual of your own invention or, following the example of various cultures, take a few moments to light a candle, burn incense, or cleanse the vibration of the room using a smudge stick made of sage. One ritual or ceremony is not superior to another despite the insistence of many zealous practitioners who believe their way is the best. You are the master of your own destiny and can create the ideal vibration using your own intuition and feelings as a guide. Trust the process.

Purpose

When you are ready to place a cure, remember the reasons you have chosen to focus on this particular aspect of your life and environment. If it is your intention to bring into your room and life the absent energies symbolized by Earth, keep this purpose clearly in your mind as you install the cure. Return to the Visualization Process Worksheet in Chapter 4 and use the text you have filled in to guide you. What you create in your life will depend upon *how* you install the cure, and to what degree you allow your purpose to be embraced by *possibility*. If you place a mirror on a wall where you have identified negative space, and as you are hammering in the nails, you are thinking, "This is never going to work, but what the heck—let's give it a try," at best you will have limited results. However, if you recite or see, in your mind's eye, the positive, life-changing affirmation you have written in the Visualization Process Worksheet for this particular house of the bagua that has been creating difficulty, the cure will be far more likely to achieve the purpose you desire.

In Intuitive Feng Shui, you are not simply changing your environment, you are transforming your life. Both your thoughts and the cures carry vibration. Changing places means first changing vibrations. Remember, *image precedes matter.* Embrace possibility!

The Cures

Looking glass upon the wall, who is fairest of them all?
GRIMM'S FAIRY TALES

Mirrors

While watching a magician saw a woman in half or make an elephant vanish in midair, the baffled spectator can hardly imagine just how simple these illusions really are. Without mirrors, more than half the magic of Las Vegas would be lost. Alice in Wonderland discovered a whole new world beyond the looking glass, and Snow White's fate was closely tied to the mirror on the wall. Because mirrors are one of the most commonly employed cures in feng shui, it is important to understand how to use them properly.

Mirrors for Simple Reflection

Mirrors have many different functions. As an ordinary object, the mirror reflects the human image and is used almost every day for shaving, applying makeup, straightening neckties or hemlines, and dressing. The two most common mirrors in our homes, in the bedroom and bath, may actually be creating difficulty while performing their basic function.

All mirrors should be kept spotlessly clean. Broken, damaged, worn, or faded mirrors will have a strong effect, usually undesirable, and should be replaced. Decorative mirrors made of smoked glass can be lovely in the right place to create a certain well-defined aesthetic feeling, but they should be avoided when the human image will be reflected amidst the haze. Similarly, painted mirrors are really objects of art and should be placed so as to function as an element of design rather than to reflect faces.

Because we are more than just our body or face, mirrors are frequently too small to reflect the whole field of energy that we really are. Around our physical body is a field of vibration called an aura. Whether we can see it or not, this field can be measured using various forms of technology, including Kirlian photography. The aura around the head, like a halo on an angel, extends about six inches beyond the physical form. When we look at our image each morning or night as it is reflected in a small bathroom mirror over the sink, who we are is limited to the physical self. Mirrors that reflect the face should be larger than the body, as we then become "larger than life."

A dressing mirror should also be large enough to include more than just the image of the physical body. Occupants of a house need to be aware of their own proportions, too, so that guests who are taller or shorter do not need to bend over or stand on tiptoes to see their reflections.

Another consideration to keep in mind is the mirror's edge. Because we know that they are made of glass, and their edges can be so razor-sharp that they could cut a finger if we rubbed the edge, mirrors should be framed, edged with a border strip, or placed flush against an adjoining perpendicular surface. By doing so, we not only eliminate the obvious safety hazard, but more important, creating the soft edge leaves only the reflective characteristic of the mirror, expanding energy, bringing more light to a corner, or creating the appearance of depth behind a counter or shelf. The cutting edge will never enter our consciousness.

Placing two mirrors side by side creates another problem. To avoid splitting the reflection with a cutting edge, use a small dividing strip of wood, fabric, or other material to mark the separation. Another option, often found in clothing stores, is to place two or more framed mirrors far enough apart so that there is at least one body's width between them. This prevents your image from appearing a third in one, a third in the other, with your "center" absent. Mirrors joined in a corner create a strange reflection, which can be circumvented by placing a large floor plant or other object at the junction point. It may be preferable to simply frame both mirrors on perpendicular walls, stopping them about twelve inches from the corner and eliminating the corner distortion completely.

A beveled-edged or etched mirror creates no problem, provided that the major portion of its reflective surface is flat. The edge acts more like a frame and can add an air of elegance to an otherwise ordinary mirror.

When two edges of a mirror are on a track, one in front of the other, like on the sliding doors on a closet, wardrobe, or medicine cabinet, they reflect images from different depths. Standing in front of this installation each morning, the first image you see of yourself looks like the face in a Picasso masterpiece, divided in the center with the depth perspective markedly different between left and right. This creates a strong imbalance that should be avoided at all costs. Even mirrors on swinging cabinet doors, though aligned on the same plane, may have a dividing line that creates a broken image of our face—and self.

Small, mirrored tiles used in a hallway, living room, or dressing area that reflect the human face or form are a feng shui nightmare, as they break images into hundreds of pieces. Used solely as a reflector of light to create a special effect, they can be eye-catching and full of sparkle, as anyone who has ever been to a discotheque would recall. In the foyer or front hall, they are unsettling—precisely the reason why the entryway of many casinos have chosen this design element. What could be better for them than to shatter your image of yourself into thousands of jagged pieces?

Mirrors should also reflect something pleasant—something worth seeing more of, like a good view, the sky, treetops, or additional light. Placing mirrors to reflect a pond or lake into the home is very auspicious. Do not place a mirror opposite the open door of the bathroom or where it reflects the garbage can. These are tired, dead, or decomposing energies that are being removed from the house, and their images should not be reflected back into the house. In the bedroom, do not place a mirror so that it reflects your image in bed. Because our ethereal energy needs rest each night too, such a placement can easily cause insomnia or poor sleep. It is fine to see a mirror from the bed, but you should not be able to see yourself when lying down. A mirror that reflects your body while sleeping will cause an expansion of vibrations, resulting in a subtle weakening of physical energy and an unnatural dream state. Because we are made of invisible vibrations, the gathering together of these energies restores us.

Mirrors in the bedroom are best when they are round or oval, creating a smoother image than those with right angles, whether square or rectangular. Circles and ovals have only one, graceful line; square or rectangular mirrors can create more conflict, especially in a small space, as the edges converge toward the corners.

Our aura, the field of vibration around us, is more spherical. A mirror reflecting our image is naturally better when it follows this form. Two intersecting lines, like those that form the corner of a square or rectangular mirror, "cross" each other in space, unlike the single, constant flow of lines in a circular or oval mirror.

The Mirror as a Cure

When used as a cure in feng shui, a properly placed mirror can create the appearance of a space where there is actually only a wall. Mirrors are used to bring negative (missing) space into the bagua. When something is missing, that is, in a floor plan in which part of the bagua has no actual living space, hanging a mirror on the wall in the room at the edge of the negative space makes that area more

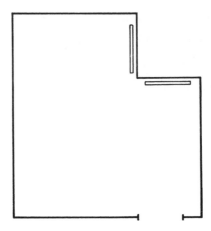

like a projection. As a result, something that was missing in space and in life appears in both.

The house of Relationships is a negative space in this floor plan. Hanging a mirror on either of the two walls that border the negative space creates an image of something there by reflecting other parts of the room into the mirror. This cure brings in Earth, the energy symbolizing partnerships, marriage, and the receptive.

Mirrors *enable energy to flow.* Placing mirrors on both sides of the main door or entryway can bring a great new flow of energy into your life. By contrast, when a door opens into a wall, as nineteenth-century European design dictated to ensure privacy, or if a corner feels cramped, chi is stagnant and unable to flow freely—the feng shui equivalent of poor blood circulation. Placed directly opposite an inner doorway leading to a small hallway, or at the bottom of a stairway where the last step ends close to a wall, a mirror creates depth. One of the most common areas where depth is restricted is the kitchen—especially behind the stove. Placing a mirror—even a small one—so that an image of depth appears rather than a flat surface will allow blocked energy to be released and open up the area with depth and light. This is an ideal cure for the tired cook who feels chained to the hot stove every day or the lonely apartment dweller who never gets any visitors.

This placement also symbolically dou-bles the number of burners on the stove, an auspicious enhancement that strength-ens health and prosperity.

In a narrow hallway or smaller space, *mirrors expand.* The little neighborhood café with only eight tables can appear to seat twice or three times as many customers if the owners have placed mirrors properly. Diners will feel less cramped and more relaxed as a result of the expanded image. Imagine how you'd feel in an airplane lava-tory were it not for the mirror on the wall; it's really a tiny box you are standing in! When a passageway seems cramped or lim-ited, it is better to place a mirror along one

137

Convex Mirror

wall than to hang a still-life painting, which would define the limit rather than extend it.

Convex mirrors have been used for decades to expand energy in the entryways of homes and apartments. A round convex mirror is placed directly opposite the doorway. As it is difficult to adjust a necktie or apply makeup using a convex mirror, this placement was obviously chosen to spread light and energy rather than merely to reflect faces.

Office

A mirror can also be used to define space, as in some open floor plans. A number of mirrors along a wall, together with plants used as dividers, make it unnecessary to erect walls or other solid partitions to delineate an area. The image reflected in the mirror is expanded and defined by placement.

An unusual but effective use of a mirror as a cure in feng shui is when strong downward energy looms over a house, apartment, or office. The source of this energy may be a large television antenna,

Terrace

a skyscraper, or a water tower. The downward energy needs to be reversed and sent upward, harmlessly diminishing its oppressive force. Mounting a concave mirror on top of the building, on the terrace, or outside the home will invert the image, dispersing and neutralizing its effect.

Round silver balls made from sterling, aluminum, or glass will reflect energy away from a window and should be used instead of a mirror when negative or cutting chi is pointed toward the opening. The effects of sharp roof lines, corners of nearby outbuildings, or other exterior offenses, including roads aimed directly at the home or office, can be harmlessly dispersed and eliminated by hanging the ornament in the window. The ideal position is slightly above eye level at an angle of about 15 degrees.

The small octagonal mirror displaying the bagua and the trigrams of the *I Ching* is often used in classical feng shui in the Far East. It is also used to disperse negative energy coming toward the house, much as other cultures would place a God's eye, mandala, or other hex sign to ward off evil. Seen through the eyes of the Unifying Principle, all these applications do the same thing: they reflect the image back, up, and out through color, light, pattern, or other means of expanding vibration. The appropriate use of this cure depends entirely upon your aesthetic design choices and an understanding of chi energy—not on some mystical, secret powers embodied in the bagua mirror, mandala, or God's eye. In fact, using something outside your own design aesthetic may cause more difficulties. In order to practice feng shui, there is no need to make your space resemble an Asian restaurant, full of tin wind chimes and bagua mirrors, unless they harmonize with your environment or you choose them as an element of design. The principles of energy and change are not limited by culture but are present in all traditional philosophies.

CASE HISTORY

The Problem: Highly cultured and refined in every way, Lady S. lived among fine antiques in a beautiful Victorian home, all of which she had inherited from her grandfather, a former member of Parliament. A close friend informed Lady S. that negative forces known as cutting chi were attacking her front door because she lived at the top of a T-junction.

The Solution: Eager to correct the problem, Lady S. asked her friend for a solution and was given a Chinese bagua mirror with the eight signs of the trigrams around the perimeter. She was instructed to place this mirror on her front door. A few weeks later, not at all convinced that the problem was solved, she had become rather distressed at the effect this placement was having and sought out the advice of an Intuitive Feng Shui consultant. Upon seeing the mirror, the consultant asked her why she had placed it there. "Well, I have cutting chi coming right in my front door," she replied, wondering why the consultant would ask such a silly question when the offensive energy was so obvious. "Yes, I can see that," he replied, "but what has happened since you have placed it there?" Lowering her voice and changing her tone, Lady S. confessed, "Well, to be perfectly honest with you, the only thing that I've noticed is that everyone who comes now asks, 'What is that thing doing here?'"

The Result: The consultant then noted how completely out of character this cure was for Lady S., who was standing there in a dark blue suit, a proper white-lace-collared blouse, and a full set of pearls around her neck. Inside the home, he found lovely period furnishings, very British in origin. He recommended that she remove the bagua mirror and in its place

put a shiny, brass door knocker, convex and polished, which would both harmonize with and protect her lovely home. Lady S. was delighted at the elegant new fixture on her front door, a cure that matched her lifestyle and resonated in *her* world.

All healing forces must be within, not without!
The applications from without are to create within
a coordinating mental and spiritual force.
EDGAR CAYCE

Clear as Crystal

A sparkling crystal, a flicker of light—a rainbow of color! Crystals appear magical to young and old alike. From the earliest of times, human beings have been fascinated with the world of minerals— and why not? We are made up of millions of crystal elements, minerals in our cells, glistening deep within us like the heavenly bodies above us. Our fascination with the stars, the planets, and outer space constantly parallels our inner cosmic search.

Crystals have an extraordinary capacity to *activate energy.* Living elements, these minerals are vehicles of healing, power, good luck, and spiritual wisdom. The current appreciation of the power of these minerals is hardly something new; most cultures have a deep understanding of, and relationship with, the earth and its elements.

In Intuitive Feng Shui, there are two distinctly different categories of crystals, both of which may be used as cures to activate chi. The first group consists of clear crystals, most often faceted, the most powerful of which are diamonds. Unfortunately, these are the most expensive. Diamonds are charged with a particular meaning or purpose, like love, marriage, or ideals so elevated that we characterize them as irreplaceable. Wars have broken out over such precious objects, and countless tales of intrigue, conquest, and death have accumulated in their history. In earlier times, when kings and queens wore their crowns while strolling through the villages, their heads were in fact often adorned by a kind of traveling bagua—their presence acting as the Tai Chi. Wherever they went, *they* were the center. The eight-sided crown, with its faceted jewels of every color, served as a symbol of their spiritual power and control. The wise man, or wizard, often carried a staff topped with a round crystal, another symbol of magic over the mortal souls who sought his counsel. Today, some feng shui consultants, like the wizards of old, employ the same accoutrements as they perform their duties.

For those with unlimited financial resources, no feng shui cure can be as powerful as a properly placed, flawless diamond to activate chi in an environment. But because few people can be expected to hang diamonds in their windows, a clear, manmade crystal is a perfectly acceptable alternative. Crystals on stands placed on side tables or bookshelves achieve the same results.

The glitter produced by a chandelier in the center of the grand ballroom draws us to the light. The faceted glass cover of a small candle on the table causes the flame within to sparkle and illuminate the area in a special way. A teardrop-shaped pendulum or faceted round orb hung in a window refracts the light, sending out rays of color into the room. All of these are examples of crystals activating chi.

In some cases where negative space appears, a window prevents the installation of a mirror. Instead, hang a crystal in the center of the window. It will activate the chi that was missing and bring it into the room and your life.

It is best to choose partially or fully faceted glass crystals that are symmetrical—like orbs, diamond shapes, or teardrops—rather than a crystal shaped like a swan or a horse, which is more an object of art. Asymmetrical faceted glass objects can create imbalance. In most cases, a small crystal, not much larger than a cherry, will be more than enough to achieve the desired effect. Tennis-ball-sized faceted crystal balls can be used for dining rooms seating a hundred people, not ten. Immense glass crystals can cause the electromagnetic waves of light to vibrate so intensely that you might find yourself replacing light bulbs or fuses instead of activating harmonious energy in your bedroom.

Small crystals can also be installed where there is no window in order simply to activate energy in the related house of the bagua. Even the tiny sparkle they produce will draw energy into the area, subconsciously activating energy in the related aspect of our lives.

The other crystals that can be used in feng shui are those made of raw minerals such as amethyst, tourmaline, rose quartz, and others. These organic minerals carry a certain charge that can be associated with the different organs, emotions, and other elements in our lives. After careful study of their properties, you may wish to use these beautiful objects as another way to affect the vibrational world. They are potentially extremely powerful, so it is important to recognize that they need to be well cared for and treated with respect. They should be cleaned every week or two in fresh water *without* salt (use of which will cause microscopic damage) and allowed to air dry, preferably in fresh air and sunlight. Much has been written elsewhere about the unusual characteristics and proper care of these types of crystals. As feng shui cures, large crystals of this type can be placed on shelves or countertops or by the bedside to activate chi in that area. Other effects are not specifically related to placement but come from the inherent properties of the crystals, which you can investigate more deeply if you are interested.

The Nature of Crystals

Manmade crystals are perfectly symmetrical and uniform, much like processed bread or assembly-line computer chips. Crystals, bread, and computer chips each carry a vibration as well as a material form. Although their beauty is wonderful to behold, crystals most often used in Intuitive Feng Shui are powerful and important more because of what is carried in them—the invisible part—rather than what they look like. Certainly it is important that clear glass balls like those found on a chandelier be flawless, shiny intensifiers of light and chi, pleasing to look at and enjoy. But success in using these objects has more to do with visualization when they are used than with their size, shape, or appearance.

In nature, crystals occur in infinite variety, like snowflakes or leaves. No two examples are alike. Naturally occurring crystal is ideally used in Intuitive Feng Shui because no two situations that call for the use of a crystal are alike.

Another important reason these crystals are so powerful is that their geometry aligns with the magnetic fields of the earth. Aware that we are placing a divine object more than 100 million years old helps us relate to the infinite much more easily than when working with a 30 mm glass crystal from a mail-order company or the local jeweler. Glass crystals have become quite common; nature crystals will remain unique eternally.

The use of crystals has a long, honorable history; they have been employed for sacred purposes by most of the world's religions. Native Americans, Buddhist monks, and shamanic healers have used crystals, as have their counterparts in the Judeo-Christian traditions. Crystals carry the energy of possibility, a key component of Intuitive Feng Shui practice.

Crystals worn as jewelry affect the vibrational field around the body. When they are worn constantly, they create a certain energy and charge. With wise use, you may learn to tap into the subtle yet profound healing qualities they possess. Without knowing what effect a particular piece of jewelry may be having, however, you may be creating a subtle imbalance with a necklace or bracelet you rarely remove. Experiment with crystal jewelry, and see if you can notice how the energy of one piece may "charge" you while another may drain your energy.

Clear Quartz The use of clear quartz crystal can bring a greater clarity to mind and body. It is most beneficial in cases where general physical healing is needed, when occupants have low energy, or when a project or effort needs a particular boost. It can be used in any area of the bagua. Choose examples with the fewest scratches or least wear, preferably with perfect points. Those containing small "imperfections" that reveal refraction of light and cause a rainbow effect are especially potent.

Rose Quartz Rose quartz crystal is perfect to promote harmony in relationships, heal old emotional wounds, overcome anger, and bring a general state of calm into a space where relationships are of particular importance. They are especially helpful in the house of Earth.

This crystal is often referred to as the "heart opener" and can stimulate general well-being and a feeling of love in both man and woman. It is widely available, inexpensive, and quite beautiful used on a desktop, shelf, or counter.

Amethyst Amethyst crystal has the capacity to purify the etheric body, which nourishes the heart and blood. It is particularly helpful when there is an excess of stress and, of course, is best placed in the house of Fire. Amethyst can also heighten the feminine nature, helping those who use it to have a deeper experience of the nature of Soul. It is often thought to be most aligned with the quality of personal illumination due to the deep silver hue within the crystal. The hue mirrors the self, reflecting God in the subtle world.

This crystal has the unique quality of transmutation and integration: that is, when used properly, it brings intellect into harmony with direct experience. It is especially beneficial in coordinating all seven chakras and can be used with clear quartz crystal most effectively.

Malachite Malachite crystal is much like chlorophyll in the plant world, carrying life force to deeper places fed by smaller veins and capillaries. Malachite is an extraordinarily nourishing crystal capable of tuning one into the nurturing and warming aspects of the parent and family. It is best used in the house of Thunder, closely related to our elders and protection. In extreme cases, this crystal can also help rid the body of excess radiation.

Malachite can be found in many different shades of green. The lighter tones relate more to recent elders, as well as to our own circulatory system and lungs, while the darker shades carry properties connected to our ancestors and our own physical heart. Malachite helps mend bones and stimulates the creation of healing tissue and cells. In such cases, or when creativity is blocked, it can be effectively placed in the house of the Lake.

Citrine Citrine stimulates the physical body with its intense yellow, orange, or golden hue. The lighter yellow shades relate more to the emotional body while darker tones connect with the physical. Citrine stimulates chi in the solar plexus, usually an area where people hold a great deal of sadness or hurt from past injury. Like malachite, this crystal is best placed either in the house of the Lake or Thunder in situations where balance is needed for past family issues or challenges with children.

Citrine can also support people in stating clearly what it is they want, as its use stimulates the throat. Its resonance varies according to the hue, so be certain that the crystal you choose is appropriate for the user.

Smoky Quartz This crystal is also used effectively in conjunction with clear quartz, creating a light/dark polarity to stimulate

149

physical manifestation. Experiment with one in each hand (try placing the smoky quartz in the left hand and the clear one in the right hand) to see if you can detect the charge.

These polarities help break apart stagnant patterns where some potential energies are being withheld or blocked. For example, if a child is doing poorly in school but clearly has the ability to do better, a teacher might comment, "Johnny is not living up to his full potential." This is an ideal use for these two crystals.

Smoky quartz alone brings to the surface that which has been hiding underneath, allowing latent talent to manifest. Its use is far more physical in fact than emotional, causing something to actually appear in matter as opposed to being only sensed. Smoky quartz might help a child get that science project done, but wouldn't be particularly helpful in getting the child to stand up in class and answer a question. This crystal creates matter in the physical realm, dissolving obstructions and encouraging flow.

It is best used moderately in the house of Water. Be careful that its placement is not reflected in a mirror. More than any other type of crystal, it needs to be well cared for and cleaned often, as much as once a week.

Tourmaline This is an unusual crystal that can occur in many different colors. As such, it is strongly linked to creativity and divine manifestation. Many channelers and healers use tourmaline to open themselves to a higher source. It is often referred to as the "Christ Stone" for its ability to help us rise above the mundane matters of the world and reflect the Divine in our work on earth.

Fine specimens of tourmaline are usually quite expensive and often used in jewelry. When placed in the house of the Mountain, this crystal connects with the higher self and has the potential to facilitate a deeper sense of love of self.

Examples called "rainbow tourmaline" or "watermelon tourmaline" have particularly high polarities within them, strongly stimulating the third-eye chakra.

Rhodochrosite An exquisite salmon-colored crystal, rhodochrosite is among the most overlooked yet powerful substances to use in personal transformation. Though directly related to the nervous system, this crystal actually carries a powerful aura-sealing energy that protects the etheric body. In the next lesson, together with one assignment on the aura, more specific information concerning the use of this crystal will be presented.

Rhodochrosite is not easily found in large quantities, as the sources of this unusual stone are becoming depleted. Over time, practitioners of Intuitive Feng Shui have become more familiar with the various qualities of this and many other crystals by carefully experimenting with them in their own lives and spaces. Their personal experiences make it possible for them to offer, with integrity, their knowledge of crystals.

Crystals and the Tai Chi

It is possible to place a crystal in any of the eight areas of the bagua, or even a number of crystals in many areas. They can be used effectively alone or with other feng shui cures; however, when placing a crystal in the Tai Chi, it is wise to remove other cures, like mirrors or wind chimes, from the immediate environment, as they will create further imbalance rather than solve a problem. After many months of unsuccessfully trying various cures to change some aspect of the bagua, you can place a crystal in the Tai Chi that will change the *whole* bagua, rotating it imperceptibly as the crystal spins on its string. This is a very powerful cure and usually causes a noticeable transformation of chi in the area and in one's life. It should be used only as a last resort to achieve a desired result, as subtle changes may actually have a more enduring impact.

The light of the body is the eye: if therefore thine eye be single, thy whole body shall be full of light.

MATTHEW 6:22, KING JAMES VERSION

Lights

The Unifying Principle seeks the merging of opposites. Spiritual teachers from Lao Tsu to Jesus and scriptures from the Qur'an to the *Pearls of Wisdom* speak of joining the "two eyes of man" into one for enlightenment. In feng shui, *light is energy,* and the addition of properly placed lighting fixtures not only changes the ambiance or mood of a room but also enhances the related symbolic aspects of the house of the bagua in which they are installed.

Light can be used as a cure in many different ways. Glare, shadows, and overly bright bulbs can create an unstable environment. With indirect lighting, by contrast, the fixtures are hidden but the light they create can be adjusted to fill a room. This kind of lighting may be far easier to control, with a minimum of negative effects.

Modern studies of emotional disorders caused by lack of light show that profound healing could take place when light is added to a dark environment. New technologies now offer full-spectrum and color-corrected instruments to replace outmoded fluorescent fixtures that cast pale, ghostly shadows in eerie hallways. Chapter 16, on feng shui and ecology, goes into this area in greater detail.

Where negative space has been identified, light can bring the missing area back into the bagua. This is possible only when the area is outside the home or work environment and the occupant is able to place a light at the imaginary corner created by the existing structure. Ideally, the fixture should be aimed so that it floods the negative space with light.

In such cases, an outdoor spotlight can be aimed back at the house to illuminate the missing area, as in the example above where Mountain is a negative space. This activates the part of the bagua that symbolizes Contemplation.

Fixtures positioned on the floor or ceiling close to the wall that they illuminate can be used to wash the wall with light and bring energy to the area. Up- or down-lights can be used effectively to illuminate plants, wall hangings, art, and other objects in a room. Indirect fixtures and task lighting can eliminate glare or soften an environment, or they can provide what's needed for specific purposes with dramatic results.

For most people, candlelight is more romantic than any other option. White or natural beeswax candles are best suited for this purpose; colored candles may produce less-harmonious environments and those containing paraffin release carcinogenic elements into the environment.

Any area of the bagua, even when it is not a negative space, will be affected by the addition of light. If you wish to activate or charge a particular area, place a floor or table lamp in the house of the bagua you want to "cure," particularly if it is obviously in need of some bright energy!

Bright Objects

Mirrors, crystals, and lights are all "bright objects" and are used to add positive, active energy. Bright objects with reflective qualities add the beauty of artistic design, the softer nature of fabric as opposed to glass or metal, and the possibility of a wide range of color. These objects may be modern or traditional tapestries with small, shiny disks or sequins woven into the fabric, or wall hangings made of fibers or collage with sparkling threads, foil, or specks of glitter in the design. Placing sparkling objects of this type on a wall can be an effective cure for negative space or can be used to activate energy in a particular house of the bagua. Even a color or black-and-white photograph of a majestic waterfall or sparkling mountain stream can be considered a bright object that will activate chi.

Wind Chimes

Understanding that the proper placement of any object in an environment will influence the world of vibrations, occupants of a home or office must also consider the major role sound waves can play in feng shui. As one of the classical cures, a wind chime is used to *moderate or change chi flow* and marks a point where distinctly different energies converge. For example, wind chimes are often placed above the main entrance of a store or restaurant. The purpose is more than just to announce the visitor; in fact, the air current causes an audible response, subtly telling those who pass by it that "you are now leaving the traffic and outdoor noise of the city and entering the quiet, refined ambiance of our fine establishment: lower your voice and change your energy accordingly." Wind chimes have the same

effect of distinguishing two different energies when positioned between the kitchen and dining room of a restaurant or home. In some cultures, beaded curtains accomplish the same results.

Wind chimes are available in a wide variety of different shapes, sizes, and materials as well as varying pitch, sound quality, and harmony. Because sound waves resonate differently with each individual, it is wise to listen to a wind chime or bell before purchasing or installing it. Be careful when ordering chimes online; they may look far more beautiful than they sound. Fortunately, many of the best sources give you the option to listen to their chimes as well as look at their images. The correct wind chime for your home is the one that sounds right to you. Beauty is in the eyes *and ears* of the beholder.

In homes where the front door is exactly opposite the back door, and the hallway in between has no obstruction or fixture to break the flow of energy, place a wind chime anywhere it feels suitable in order to moderate the flow and prevent vital life force from escaping. In long hallways or corridors, particularly where there are a number of doorways or arches, placing a wind chime in between one or more of the openings moderates energy and gently transforms one long tunnel into a few different areas of passage.

As cures used to treat specific houses of the bagua, wind chimes have a similar, moderating effect when placed inside a room. This is especially helpful when the energy of one house is disturbed or disrupted by events in life. For example, if you find yourself engaged in a family dispute with your parents or an ongoing argument with your spouse, wind chimes placed in Thunder and Earth, respectively, will help to change the energy, potentially pacifying the opposing forces.

A wind chime is used in two ways for protection from negative energy entering a home or office. The first is to install a wind chime or bell in a window facing the force, thereby changing the way in which occupants will receive the incoming energy. Unlike the round, silver ball that reflects and disperses energy, a wind chime used in this way changes it, reducing its negativity but not eliminating it completely. This placement would be ideal when a neighbor *sometimes* plays loud music, or patrons of a nearby bar or pub become rowdy late at night. These energies are natural and living, albeit bothersome, so reducing or moderating them with a wind chime is more appropriate than repelling them completely with a silver orb.

The second use for a wind chime is to protect from the constantly moving force often referred to as "the dragon"—signified by the number five in the bagua. In feng shui astrology, this force changes position every year. Installing a chime and orienting it toward this force provides protection. For example, in 2010, the dragon sits in the southwest, while in 2011, it moves to the east. Fine tuning a property in this way may require the advice of a knowledgeable, qualified practitioner, so the chime is properly repositioned each year.

Other Sounds, Music, and Noise

Abrasive, electronic sounds like that of an elevator door kept open too long create discordant energy that irritates the nervous system. Some alarm clocks are highly effective for just this reason: we can't wait to stop the noise! And when passing through a doorway breaks a silent beam of light, which in turn causes an annoying and loud "eehhngnnngnnngng," anyone in earshot would prefer a more pleasant natural chime or bell to the electronic alternative.

Music has long been shown to be an effective way to alter behavior and can be included with wind chimes and bells as an element altering the vibrational world of space. When an argument with a parent or elder persists, and the stereo system in your home is located in Thunder, it may be far more beneficial to change from discordant rock music to the more peaceful nocturne or folk song than to hang a wind chime there. Feng shui is a way of examining all things that affect our senses, so it is as imperative to be aware of the importance of music and the element of sound as it is to harmonize the world of color and light.

Both high- and low-frequency vibrations, commonly "unheard" until they cease, can cause considerable stress and irritation to occupants of a home or office. Most background noise originates from electronic devices, ventilation equipment, and ordinary appliances. Refrigerator compressors cycle on and off more than a dozen times each day. Elevators hum, heat pumps rumble, and hard drives buzz so imperceptibly that we may not notice them until they stop. We then sit in awe of the true silence behind the noise.

Sound machines, emulating rushing water and other natural phenomena, mask these irritants but do not always neutralize them. Incorporating soft tapestries as wall hangings or fresh plants that absorb and balance these unnatural energies can soften environments where these background noises exist. Although the effects of background radiation have been well documented, we are only just beginning to understand how harmful the constant presence of extreme sound waves can be to our health. Electronic smog is discussed in greater detail in Chapter 15.

Plants and Flowers

There is no better way to harmonize the external and internal environment than to include plants in the interior design plan. Shape, symbolism, and sunlight, as well as color, all play a role in selecting the right plant. As a rule, almost all living plants and fresh flowers *bring auspicious energy* to a room and help to *stimulate activity* in the associated house of the bagua. The few exceptions are culturally specific. The occupants' beliefs and preferences should be honored. Not doing so can lead to a mismatch of the ancient Chinese choices with another culture's taboos.

CASE HISTORY

The Problem: Madam H., the wife of a Greek industrialist, was completing the renovation of their palatial estate outside Athens when she heard about feng shui. She was able to contact a master in Hong Kong, to whom she sent a complete set of plans. Upon receiving them back, she instructed her groundskeeper and gardeners to follow the expert's directions, which included installing a row of rubber tree plants between the main house and a reflecting pool. During the weeks that followed, her entire staff resigned, and to her utter amazement, a large celebration she had planned had to be canceled not only because of the lack of help but because of guests whose "plans changed at the last minute," causing them to renege on their prior acceptance.

The Solution: Madam H. called in an Intuitive Feng Shui consultant who reviewed the plans. Suspecting that the choice of plants may have been culturally specific, he contacted a friend familiar with Greek culture. "Rubber tree plants are bad luck," he was told—a belief in sharp contrast to the Chinese position, which considers the plant to be very auspicious. Investigating the matter herself, Madam H. discovered that her groundskeeper had kept this information from her out of respect, but his colleagues all had become frightened at what might happen after the plants were installed. Furthermore, the employees of the nursery where the plants were purchased had been aghast at this order from such a respectable family and began to gossip about the difficulties that were certain to befall the household. Gardeners from other households heard the sad tale, exaggerated it to catastrophic proportions, and told their employers. Before long, tall tales of grave misfortune were being whispered among the householders, each one deciding to decline the invitation to the party rather than risk bad luck by attending.

The Result: Madam H. called her former staff to a meeting and explained what had happened. They removed the plantings, replacing them with flowering bushes symbolizing peace. The correction was redirected into the gossip pipeline, and a very successful, grand event was held a month later with her entire staff present and the guest list complete.

Keep Plants Healthy!

Healthy plants are wonderful additions to houses of the bagua that need strengthening or improving. They must be tended to properly, however, because if they are not they can cause deterioration of energy as they wither. Larger plants have more chi.

Hanging plants, ivies, and creeping vines need to be well cared for, as they may appear to people as invaders rather than welcome design elements.

The sharply pointed leaves of a palm or other semitropical plant need plenty of room to prevent their cutting energy from piercing the psyche of a person sitting in a chair or couch nearby.

In small areas, plants with rounded leaves create less cutting chi, which can cause subtle discomfort.

Beware of cacti in cramped areas; they grow in the huge expanse of a desert and thus are inappropriate for use in tight corners. Their needles send a subconscious wave of anxiety to those nearby.

Dried floral arrangements, including amber-colored leaves and evergreens, are appropriate seasonally and are best avoided in the spring and summer months.

Plastic or other artificial plants should be avoided unless there is absolutely no other alternative. In such cases—for example, where a good light source is unavailable or occupants suffer extreme allergic reactions to live plants or flowers—artificial substitutes should be of the highest quality and placed "out of reach." Using artificial plants that do not activate chi is more the work of a decorator than someone skilled in feng shui.

A beautiful potted plant or hanging basket can transform a high-pressure work environment into a more peaceful one by contributing oxygen and negative ionization to the atmosphere. As an expression of gratitude or friendship, a lovely plant or fresh flowers are a far more positive offering than a box of chocolates!

Water, Fountains, Pools, and Fish Tanks

As both the literal and symbolic source of life, Water is a key element in feng shui. Our biological evolution began in salt water, and our existence prior to life in air depended upon the quality of the water environment in our mothers' wombs. The symbolism of Water is explored throughout this book; water as an element of design, or for use as a cure in feng shui, is particularly important to understand.

Water *is* life and should flow toward us without obstruction.

In early cultures, where placement was common sense and the need for clean water essential to life, houses were sited near good sources of water, their front doors facing in the direction of water flowing toward them. Underground energies, as well as those in the vibrational world, would therefore bring auspicious energy and vital life force to the occupants, resulting in good fortune. To enhance this energy, or to create it when it was notably absent, shop owners would commonly place a small fountain or stream near the entry-way, the direction of flowing water running parallel to the path leading into the home or shop. This type of placement is frequently seen in the foyer of Asian restaurants where diners enter.

In classical feng shui, water also symbolizes good fortune. Aquariums with a precise number of fish (nine orange and one black) are commonly placed near the cash register in stores or restaurants, recommended to increase wealth.

Clear, still water can be useful in balancing negativity, where confusion and tension are present. Embodying the opposite energy of Fire, water can be used as a cure when an environment becomes too highly charged as a result of human or design elements in conflict. The cooling, passive nature of water will neutralize excess Fire energy.

In contrast, water can also *activate energy,* for example, with the installation of a small fountain or water sculpture. This can be done in any house of the bagua. A bubbling aquarium complete with goldfish is an example of a "double" cure that incorporates both the symbolism of good fortune contained in the tank and activity expressed by the live fish.

The sound of running water can also be quite cooling, as studies have shown, and helpful in an overheated environment. This is another example of excess Fire being neutralized by adding water.

Placing a birdbath outside the home, particularly if the area is a negative space, is another way to activate the missing energy. If it is not well maintained, however, the cure may create stagnation and confusion as the water becomes dirty or full of leaves. Inside installations should be kept clean for the same reason. Water placements of any type should be avoided in the northeast corner of a home or plot.

Live Animals in the Home

Dogs, cats, birds, and other animals kept in the house or work environment bring in a very specific energy that is closely related to our own perceptions. Others might easily regard "man's best friend" as little more than a smelly nuisance. Some visitors might perceive a beautiful, rare cockatoo as a source of offensive odors. Review the First Impressions Worksheet in Chapter 6 to see what other people might be seeing that you are not.

Observe the symbolism related to animals in your house. If you are having trouble finding a mate, and your dog's favorite pillow is in the Earth corner, you may want to find another position for Fido to call home. Animals have an extraordinary capacity to sense the vibrational world and will move toward good energy even when it is not visible. A dog or cat looking for a place to lie down outside is not just looking for the most comfortable spot but one with good chi coming from the earth. Mice who abandon a ship while it's docked at port, or who suddenly leave a house for no apparent reason, are sensing approaching danger. Many times, their departure is followed closely by catastrophe.

Domesticated animals need not be replaced by symbolic feng shui cures. Their place in the home or business environment should simply be taken into consideration on the vibrational and symbolic as well as the practical level.

Artwork, Sculpture, Photography

If there were an operative principle when choosing art for the home or office, it would have to be "I don't know anything about art, but I know what I like." Whether the picture you hang on the wall is an abstract "flower" by your four-year-old or a vase of sunflowers by

Van Gogh, the art you select contributes to the energy and aesthetic of place as well as the symbolism and intent of purpose.

If you hang a beautiful picture of a bullfighter in Thunder, don't be surprised if you are in conflict with your parents; correspondingly, if you wish to stimulate the energy of relationships and marriage characterized by the house of Earth in the bagua, it is helpful to place there art symbolizing pairs of objects, couples, or something with beautiful imagery. Remove the single candlestick or the photo of the lone wanderer on the beach from the house of Earth, regardless of their aesthetic quality. Art is an external expression of our inner world.

The visual energy of art can have a tremendous influence on the way in which we experience an environment. To be surrounded by photographs of birds in flight, hot air balloons or kites, and tall palm trees raises our chi. Oil paintings of landscapes or oceans expand chi in a room, while still lifes and portraits tend to be more two-dimensional and flat, thereby minimizing the expansive feeling that may be needed. Abstract and modernistic pieces without a focus will create an environment in which the occupants may find it difficult to complete things.

Wooden and metal sculptures may appear either delicate or solid and should be chosen with their symbolism clearly in mind. Sharply pointed extensions may create cutting chi and need to be placed accordingly. Smooth surfaces, complex patterns, fine detailing, and other features will affect the way in which we perceive every work of art in relation to our lives. The way colors in art affect our internal and external environment is discussed in Chapter 12.

Solid and Heavy Objects

Solid objects in our environment bring energies *downward and inward.* Used as cures in a particular house of the bagua, a solid or heavy mass will "ground" what is already happening or stabilize a precarious situation. If your job is on the line, or your relationship is in doubt, placing an overstuffed armchair in Water and Earth, respectively, will help. In contrast, when something in your life is "stuck" and seems immovable, like a heavy rock, observe where in your home or workplace heavy objects may be contributing to the impasse.

Mass creates waves in the vibrational world. Standing in a room blindfolded, you can sense the difference between an immense object, like a solid, metal block the size of a piano, and a light, porous article, like a wicker basket full of feathers. Although they occupy the same space, the energy they create in waves around their physical form is very different. The temperature in a room made of stone and ceramic tiles may be the same as one made of wood, but it *feels* colder when the density of mineral is experienced in comparison to bamboo flooring.

Dependence upon vision can limit our ability to sharpen our other senses. It is not unusual to discover musicians or others with a highly developed sense of sound to have impaired or no sight. Many of the world's greatest composers were blind, as are a disproportionate number of piano tuners. Blindfolded, a sighted person must begin to see with the other senses to compensate quite naturally for the absence of vision.

It is this invisible world of vibration that first tells us that solid, heavy objects are what they are; then, using vision, we process what we "know" to be true, deepening our experience of weight, density, and other qualities by drawing from our past experience.

To train yourself in sensing vibration without dependence upon vision, try the exercise that follows.

SENSORY EXERCISE

Purpose: To help you recover your innate ability to detect the world of vibrations without the help of visual perception.

Go with a friend to a large museum, carrying with you a good blindfold that will completely cover your eyes. Take along a notebook and pencil to record your results. After you are inside, but before you enter any of the galleries, place the blindfold over your eyes, and allow your friend to be your guide, using the following list of opposites as a checklist:

_____	Solid, heavy	_____	Hollow, light
_____	Up	_____	Down
_____	Live vibrations	_____	Electric vibrations
_____	Blocked	_____	Unobstructed
_____	Corner	_____	Open

Instruct your guide to place you directly in a variety of places, distinguished by the quality of energy. It is not necessary to follow any particular order through this test. For example, the guide should put you in the middle of a room, where there is nothing in front of you, and ask you to "feel" this. Then, the guide should place you one to three feet away from a huge marble or bronze sculpture, like a Rodin or Henry Moore piece, and ask you to "feel" this, not telling you what is there. Then move on to a vase of flowers on display in the lobby, or stand directly in front of a tall plant; after that, go to an elevator door or an electrical panel and feel the energy around you.

Next, have your guide lead you to the stairway, stopping just short of the first step. The energy that flows up the stairs will feel considerably different from the energy that flows down. You know this through an instinctual, non-visual perception, as you are still blindfolded, rather than through any of your other four senses.

Finally, let yourself be guided to a corner where two solid, blank walls meet. Then have your guide place you in front of an open window, or at a balcony, where there is only unobstructed space immediately in front of you.

Developing the senses may take some time, so don't be discouraged if you have difficulty at first in distinguishing up from down or heavy from light. As your environment (both inner and outer) becomes more clear, you will be surprised at how easy it is to "sense" what you thought you have only been seeing.

Chapter 11

How Am I Doing?

There is nothing wrong with change, if it is in the right direction.
WINSTON CHURCHILL

Do *not* underestimate the power of the changes that may occur as a result of practicing feng shui. The following story may remind you to explore more carefully, and with greater respect, the invisible world of energy that is affected by installing cures in your environment.

At the beginning of an intermediate course on Intuitive Feng Shui, participants were asked to share their experiences with the rest of the group. Amazing stories of new romances, job offers, family reconciliations, and increased wealth filled the room. Most students had gone home after the introductory course three months earlier and transformed their lives with what they had learned. One man, however, who appeared quite troubled after hearing of everyone else's successes, stood up and shared a considerably different experience that shocked the group. "After the introductory weekend, I was so excited that I went right home and made a lot of changes. In the weeks that followed, my life was filled with disaster. I changed a lot of the cures, but things kept happening that seemed to come from what I was doing. One of my children fell down the stairs and broke her arm, our refrigerator compressor froze up and needed to be replaced at huge expense, my wife had a brief affair, I was laid off from my job, and there was a small fire in my workshop. I came back to this course to find out what I did wrong and how to get back my normal life again!"

With jaws dropped, other participants questioned him about what adjustments he had made. He went over the long list of changes, including hanging crystals in windows, placing mirrors and wind chimes, painting walls, moving furniture, replacing artwork, and installing cures that he had invented. He admitted that he'd neither cleared the space nor paid attention to the visualizations, but this was not the reason why things had gone so wrong. One student finally asked him the right question: "What was wrong?" "That's just it," he responded quickly. "My life was great! I had a good job, a happy marriage, healthy children, and a good income. I thought things would get better!" An old woman jumped to her feet. "If it ain't broke, don't fix it!" she yelled.

The man in the example was "changing" success and happiness to its complementary opposite—failure and misery. The installation of one or two carefully placed cures will improve even the happiest, most successful life. At the beginning, less is more. Just go slowly if you are already close to where you want to be, and don't overdo it. Intuitive Feng Shui can have powerful results, like any other practices, if approached recklessly or without respect for the invisible world of vibrations.

Evaluating What You Have Done

Here is where the priorities list you created in Chapter 4 can be quite useful. Address the areas of concern you have in your life with these priorities clearly in mind. Don't be greedy about money, for example, if you have a pretty good cash flow but simply want more. Chances are that changing a related area that involves far greater difficulty will also improve other parts of your life. Getting into a good relationship leading to marriage might double your income!

Move slowly, placing only one or two cures at a time. In this way, you will be better able to determine the cause of what is happening. Hanging mirrors or crystals all over the house may change things, but it will be very difficult to trace the source cure. If you happen to make a mistake and place a cure incorrectly, a small problem may arise that will tip you off to the error. If the mirror is put in the wrong place first, a major catastrophe will not occur, nor is it likely that things will improve.

How to Tell if Energy Is Changing

Small improvements should become apparent almost immediately, and at the latest, after one full phase of the moon has passed, about twenty-eight days. Reflect at that time on what you have noticed. Has one of your poems been published after you placed a plant in Water? Have you become pregnant after hanging a crystal in Lake? Did you break through a logjam in your relationship with your dad after hanging a mirror on the wall bordering the negative space of Thunder? Through simple self-reflection, see how your life has changed. In the months that follow your first successes, continue to move slowly through the priorities list until you reach the end. There should be a cure or adjustment installed for every house of the bagua where you have identified problems, imbalances, or difficulties in your life and space. Any area you gave a *B, C,* or *D* needs attention, but begin with the more difficult challenges.

When Things Get Worse

One of the basic laws of the Unifying Principle tells us that, at the extremes, everything changes to its opposite. A balloon will expand continuously until it bursts. A country's power will grow until it collapses. As we approach the end of a long cycle of change, things may get a bit worse before they begin to get better.

If you are certain that the adjustments you have made are correct, and you have checked and double-checked the guidelines in earlier chapters, do not remove a cure if something appears at first to get worse. The rejection notice will look better in hindsight if the next publisher accepts your poetry and wants you to sign a contract for more money. Missing the last ferry of the day turns out to be a blessing when you hear the news that it sank, although it is hard to see that when you are left stranded at the dock.

After a while, if things are clearly not improving despite your best efforts, look within. Answers to chronic problems are usually right in front of us and easily overlooked. It is more likely to be something incredibly simple than something extremely complex. Much of what remains in the rest of the book can broaden your understanding of feng shui and the many related areas of practice that can make a difference in your life. Don't give up—your relation to your environment can be seen on many different levels.

The Predecessor Law

One of the most important principles to understand in feng shui is the Predecessor Law: the overall vibration that remains in the space from those who lived there before you dictates much of what may be happening. It is beyond your ability to change through ordinary means of installing cures and studying the bagua.

If you move into a house where the previous occupants were divorced, and where the couple that lived there before that were always in conflict, then the chances that you and your mate will have difficulty are disproportionately higher than the law of averages would predict. If the company whose offices were in the space in which you are now working had serious financial troubles that ended in bankruptcy, then the space still carries this energy, making it difficult for your business to succeed.

On the other hand, if the store you are about to rent was vacated by a booming business that was forced to move to a larger location to expand their growing business, the space they leave behind carries an energy that is very auspicious for success. And if you and your new spouse see a house where a couple lived happily for twenty years, raising two healthy children from birth until they left for college, is now vacant due to their move to a smaller home, buy it—the Predecessor Law suggests that it is an ideal environment in which to raise a happy family.

In the next chapter on chi, you will learn what forces are present in your life that can change the energy of an environment. Without even knowing it, however, many homeowners discover that what is happening in their lives is a repeat of circumstances that may have taken place years—or even decades—before they moved in. Most of what has occurred will be clearly in evidence in the structure of the house. Negative space in Earth, without correction, creates an absence of the energy needed to create and support harmonious relationships. A toilet in Wind causes a loss of the energies of good fortune that, without correction, will lead to grave financial difficulties. In other words, you could be flushing your money away.

Stories of haunted houses, attic spirits, and jinxed storefronts can be easily understood through feng shui. Similarly, tales of guardian angels or houses with good vibes are examples of harmonious environments where the feng shui is most auspicious. As much a study of the invisible world of vibration as it is of the physical world of structure, the feng shui of any environment must be investigated deeply. When you discover problems that stem from a predecessor, there are ways to correct the imbalance.

Treating the Invisible

It is very likely that all you need to do to correct an existing effect will be very apparent after you look at the bagua. Many homeowners have installed mirrors or lights to correct negative space when the problems of the previous tenants could be clearly related to difficult circumstances. The familiar restaurant site that seems to change owners, and cuisine, every six months can be corrected by ordinary feng shui cures. Even very large buildings, like offices or hotels, can benefit from relatively small alterations in design by using the very basic precepts of feng shui.

CASE HISTORY

The Problem: A famous hotel in a major metropolis was unable to keep the occupancy rate high enough to turn a profit. The owners refurbished the guest rooms, created a new marketing plan with a top advertising agency, and hired a number of high-level managers to run the property. After three years, little had changed on the bottom line, so the owners decided to put the property up for sale. It was purchased by a group of investors who were aware of feng shui and saw a golden opportunity.

The Solution: The new owners wasted no time in making only one correction. They changed the placement of a pair of escalators that directly faced the front door. In the old design, the chi went straight down the stairs and out the door, an inauspicious placement that symbolizes loss of fortune. After the renovation of the entryway, the escalators were positioned at a right angle to the door, with a bubbling fountain and pool of water at the bottom. Energy was now blocked from rushing out—the experience of the predecessor—and was furthered strengthened by the additional cure of clear, flowing, contained water.

The Result: The hotel recovered from its financial difficulties and now enjoys one of the highest occupancy rates in the city. The new owners have profited enormously, their renovation costs repaid tenfold in the first two years.

If disastrous events have taken place in a home prior to your living there, it may be necessary to perform a simple but effective ritual to change the existing vibrational pattern. This process can be performed within the context of almost any religious practice as a complement to your personal beliefs. It is not intended to replace or negate any other method but to be used as a method of self-reflection and purification.

Clearing Spaces

Our dead never forget the beautiful world that gave them being. They still love its winding rivers, its great mountains and its sequestered vales, and they ever yearn in tenderest affection over the lonely-hearted living and often return to visit and comfort them.

CHIEF SEATTLE

In the late evening or very early morning, when the vibrations of society are at their lowest, take a place in the room or area of your home where you feel the "presence" of any spirit or where you sense the most discomfort. If you are unaware of such vibrations, then position yourself in the Tai Chi of the house or any main room other than the kitchen.

Sitting on a cushion or pillow on the floor, or in a chair, make your back straight and relax your shoulders. Close your eyes gently and quiet down your mind, letting go of the many small details you carry around each day. Allow thoughts like "I have to pick up the dry cleaning tomorrow" or "I must buy more paper towels" to pass through your consciousness without attachment. Let the ordinary sounds of refrigerators, clocks, and traffic come and go. Focus on your breath as it enters your nostrils and again as it leaves. Do not force anything to happen. Simply allow yourself to be still and quiet as you would in a basic meditation practice.

After a few moments of stillness, take a deep breath in through your nose, and as you exhale, make a simple tone or chant by expressing the sound "suuuuuuu." This should come very gently, without forcing, causing your throat to vibrate slightly. Continue to let thoughts come and go, and pay no attention to the constant commentator inside your head. Repeat the sound three or four times, with each exhalation.

With the next inhalation, return to a regular pattern of breathing for a minute or two, sitting silently. Slowly bring into your mind's eye words and images that you can speak aloud or think. Either way, you will be operating within the world of vibration as your thoughts and spoken words function through wavelengths.

In cases where there was a loss of life, think or say something like these three phrases:

> *Thank you very much for your life.* If you have been in this house before, or were the person who built this house, thank you for what you have done. We are grateful for the beautiful masonry you crafted around the fireplace and the

wonderful oak tree you planted in the backyard. For everything that you have done, for your many years of life here before me, from my heart I offer my thanks.

Wherever you are now, I wish you well. In the spirit world or the world of vibration, although I may not fully understand where you are or what happens when we leave this world, if you are there and here now, I hope you can be happy. May the space you are in bring you peace.

Don't worry about us—we will take care of this house now. There is no need to stay here anymore. We promise to take care of our family and ourselves, so you are free to go now. There is no need to hang around in this space that we have now occupied, so you can freely go on and feel at ease with what will take place here. We will seek to make ourselves happy and healthy without your presence. Take care and be in peace.

The exact words or images you use are not important and should be tailored to fit any circumstances about which you may be aware. All that is essential is that you perform this ritual from your heart. You may combine a prayer from your religion, or chant a particular sutra from another teaching, or read an appropriate passage from the scriptures, if you choose. It is a very simple communication with a place "beyond the veil" that exists in all our lives. You need not think of it as special or all that unusual, as you are already operating very much in the world of vibrations through the practice of feng shui. This ritual simply includes purification for a living spirit, clearing the spaces of the vibrational world much as we clear clutter from our attics. Because the problems of human lives are being addressed, it must come from the heart in order to be effective.

Sit for a few more minutes in quiet meditation and allow the images you have created to remain. As they diminish and when more mundane thoughts begin to appear, extend your arms in front of you, and clap your hands together very sharply three times, making the loudest sound you possibly can. Doing this will clear the space further, and more completely, at the end of the ritual.

When you have finished, take a very small handful of sea salt and spread it around the room, throwing it here and there without "aiming." Salt, as it is the most compact, dense ingredient we use in our everyday cooking, and can be considered one of the most important elements of life, is the exact complementary opposite of the invisible world of spirit or vibrations. Using salt in this way helps to balance a space where spiritual phenomena dominate the physical world. By spreading salt, you clear the space and balance the visible environment with the invisible world. Let the salt remain for a few days, and whenever you feel it is appropriate, simply sweep or vacuum it up. At a later time, you may wish to scatter the petals of fresh flowers around the room and light some candles to initiate a new vibration into the space. Be as organic and spontaneous as possible; there is no need to follow a script or anyone else's ceremony. Your sincere *intention* and open heart does more than any predetermined ritual or dogma.

You can easily invent similar rituals to fit different circumstances, wishing prior occupants well and pacifying or neutralizing any negative charge that remains from the predecessor. The important thing to understand is that we must become aware of what has taken place before in a space in order to avoid having catastrophe repeat itself.

The following story is a stunning example of the possible consequences of ignoring the invisible predecessor energy. It is only one of many documented cases; difficulties abound in areas where people have died unhappily.

In World War II, on a particular site in Ukraine, a bomb dropped by the Allies hit an orphanage, instantly ending the lives of hundreds of innocent children. Following this tragic event, the space was never "cleared," nor did anyone perform any type of ritual in order to free the area of the presence of "spirits" or energies trapped in this world of vibration. Years later, the government used this site to build an important structure that would provide the region with electricity.

It is known as Chernobyl.

Because feng shui originally emerged as a practice to honor the spirits of those who lived before us, it is only logical that we must acknowledge the possible presence of this world where we live or work. A simple prayer or heartfelt blessing is often all that is necessary to release negative energies we may not even know exist.

Chapter 12

Changing Places

Your sense faculties give you access to possibilities of deeper perception. Beyond ordinary perception, there is super-sound, super-smell and super-feeling existing in your state of being. These can only be experienced by training yourself in the depth of meditation practice which clarifies any confusion or cloudiness and brings out the precision, sharpness and wisdom of perception—the nowness of your world.

CHÖGYAM TRUNGPA,
THE SACRED PATH OF THE WARRIOR

Changing Perceptions

Feng shui is strongly dependent upon perception. If we feel, see, taste, or touch something, interplay between "us" and "other" begins to take place that we evaluate through the many parts of our nervous systems. Changing the environment that surrounds us changes our perception of it, whether that change occurs consciously or not. Few people "sense" the quality of energy in the air of a room with a negative ion generator. Most people do feel that the room is more clear, relaxing, stable, or energized, or they simply feel a bit better in this room than they do in an identical room that does not have an abundance of negative ions.

A white shirt, to some people and cultures, is a symbol of purity; to others, it is a symbol of death. Black may be a color of mourning or sadness for some; it may be the preferred celebratory choice, like a tuxedo or evening gown, for others. Aside from the cultural and societal conditioning with which we were raised, many other elements affect the way we perceive the world. Seen dogmatically, feng shui can appear to be nothing more than just another set of beliefs. Used as a point of reference for the individual, it cannot be considered apart from the many other factors that affect our chi and the energy we perceive through the millions of neurons in our physical bodies.

As biological beings, we are affected physiologically by color in many ways that are built into our central nervous systems from birth. But there are also learned behaviors that influence how color affects us personally. Some hospital workers cannot tolerate green tablecloths, since green reminds them of the color of their surgical gowns, often bloodstained at work. Others have early childhood associations with one or more colors that last a lifetime. These cultural realities play a large role in how we relate to the whole world of color.

What Controls Chi?

The single most powerful and important controller of chi in our world is ourselves. We are not just a bag of bones and tissues ruled by certain limiting "scientific" constructs such as calories, gravity, or other conceptual dogma. After observing a demonstration of *chi gong*, the traditional Chinese exercises to develop chi, most people clearly see that it is possible for each individual to train in one of the ancient martial arts and direct energy in ways that might seem unimaginable. Superhuman feats of strength, balance, resistance, concentration, and extrasensory perception are common among practitioners of these arts. Arising from many years of practice, these abilities confound scientists, whose laws of physics offer no explanation. Practicing feng shui leads to understanding how to work with and respect chi.

We control our own energy. By embracing a way of life that honors the very real world of invisible vibration, we can change our diet, exercise regimen, and activity in order to change the quality of our perception. The ancient Chinese, Indian, and Tibetan masters recognized the importance of diet and its relation to health; we in the Western world have only recently begun to acknowledge that. As diet and meditation practices begin to be recommended as a cure for heart disease, modern scientific research validates what has been known for thousands of years.

It is difficult to imagine using feng shui to change the external environment without addressing our own internal environment: the body and mind that give us the perception of the world in which we live. By changing the quality of our blood through a change in diet, we begin to change the very way we see the world. Our brain cells, bathed constantly by the blood we make from food, give us the vision of our everyday life. In addition to an awareness of diet, a meditation practice or similar training that is designed to free up the clutter in our brains rather than add more muscle to our bodies helps us to begin experiencing just how much control we really have over our lives. Although diet and way of life are often the most challenging elements for most people to change, it is essential to recognize the inherent limitations of feng shui adjustments in the external world absent of changes within our own bodies. We are not separate from our environment, nor is our environment separate from us. Positive changes made within, together with feng shui adjustments in our external environment, profoundly expand possibility.

Other People

Next to ourselves, the second most important thing affecting us is *other people*. Though we may be whistling a happy tune as we arrive home, we cannot help but be influenced by the energy of a depressed mate. In particular, our relationships with our parents are of profound importance because they essentially define the way we will experience other men and women in the world. Any therapeutic methodologies, be they psychological or spiritual, that can lead us to the inescapable recognition of who gave us life are worthwhile. Developing a deeper sense of gratitude and appreciation can begin to free us from the stranglehold of the innumerable stories and interpretations we have created of our lives. The biological and spiritual create an inseparable bond of energy that occurs with no greater power than between parents and children.

So to more deeply understand the transforming power of feng shui, we must also look inward, to ourselves and our own lives and energy, and to our immediate relationships with others, particularly our parents. Wind chimes and crystals, hung in exactly the right places, may increase the possibility of changing our perceptions through the change in our environment, but we would be wise to remember that self-development begins within and will really only be *supported* by what occurs in the external world.

The Importance of Symbolism

As the wise old man on the mountaintop tells the seekers who appear before him, life itself is meaningless; it has only whatever meaning we choose to give it. For the world-class tennis player, all that matters is the trophy and the winning payoff; for the grandfather, it is the photograph of his first grandson catching a striped bass; for the bride-to-be, it is the wedding ring; for the statesman, it is the pen used to sign a document. Each object carries with it huge symbolism. What matters most in our lives is what we *say* matters—not the pen, or the ring, but the significance we give the object in our minds. Behind the obvious lies the world of symbols.

When Fu Hsi watched the tortoise emerge from the river, he saw everything falling within one of the eight energies of the bagua. In the physical world, all our material possessions such as artwork, furniture, clothing, cars, houses, photographs, pets, collections, and so on—everything—can be seen as symbolizing one of the eight basic energies.

If we are looking for endurance in our relationships, for example, a photograph of a bunch of bananas is far less appropriate than a picture of a pine forest. Instinctually, although we may not consciously perceive it, we know that the pine trees are always green and will last for many years. The banana, on the other hand, will rot in a few days unless we consume it, and in either case, it won't last long.

Symbols in our home and work environment are everywhere. Their impact must be considered in feng shui when we seek to make improvements in our lives. Using the First Impressions Worksheet in Chapter 6, review your space as others see it. If you are trying to find a mate or improve your relationships, look for that single candlestick or lone pillow on the couch in Earth and replace it with paired objects. Is there an abstract painting hanging on a wall in an area where you really want focus? Does your dirty laundry pile up in a corner related to that part of your life that's giving you trouble? Does your door stick, causing you to enter through a correspondingly "stuck" house of the bagua? It is truly astounding to discover how the realities of your life manifest everywhere in symbols. Changing these energies means bringing in the symbols you want.

Creativity requires the courage to let go of certainty.
ERICH FROMM

Designing Your Own Cures

Where there is cutting chi, there is an angle that creates a sharp "point" that must be corrected. Placing a round object, like a potted plant, or soft material like cloth or ribbon over the corner will cancel this energy. When too much metal or stone is in an environment—for example, a kitchen with marble countertops and steel appliances—adding light, straw baskets, or soft flowers warms and opens up the energy of the space. In these cases, a simple application of the Unifying Principle is all that is needed.

Some rooms have low ceilings or heavy beams in which there is a strong downward energy. While a bamboo flute may be used in classical feng shui to lift chi upward, many other possibilities exist that will have the same effect. The reason the flute is placed, mouthpiece down, at a 45-degree angle underneath the beam is to give the impression that it is being used as a sort of brace, the wind passing through the flute lifting chi upward, thereby neutralizing the downward energy in the room. But in some environments, a bamboo flute is hardly an appropriate design element.

With the Unifying Principle, one can easily see that it would also be possible to place a large, reed-like plant, growing tall within the space, to achieve the identical effect. Other cures for the same problem could be a photograph of a colorful hot air balloon sailing above the sea, a gaggle of swans in flight as they take off from the ground, or a child throwing handfuls of confetti into the air at a party. All of these carry the energy and symbolism of lightness and upward energy by conveying a meaning and feeling experienced within.

These cures are equally as effective as the classical ones and are even more powerful when you invent them yourself.

A Rainbow of Colors

The visual spectrum of colors as refracted from sunlight spread into varying wavelengths measured in angstroms. The longer wavelengths, red and orange, create intensity and command attention. These vivid, hot colors have also been shown to create activity, as the matador knows very well. Colors created from shorter wavelengths, like violet, are more passive or cooling; their effect in an environment is calming.

The Five Transformations

Appearing as early as the fourth century BCE was a system of classification of energy known as the Five Elements. Translated more accurately today, the terms used to describe the movement of energy in this system might have been The Five Energies Going, as it implies movement through a continuum rather than a collection of static elements. A color is associated with each energy, but it is helpful to explain the system of these elements, called the Five Transformations, while looking at the related colors.

The energy of Water, our evolutionary and biological origin, is *floating*. Like the stillness of the late night or very early morning hours and of the winter season, the inactivity of this energy is associated with difficulty or calamity, as when water becomes stagnant or cloudy. The related colors are *blue* and *black*. Actually the absence of color, black absorbs other colors, and if used excessively in design, will create a depressing environment. Its best use is in definition, as a border or accent color edging or framing other colors. Too much

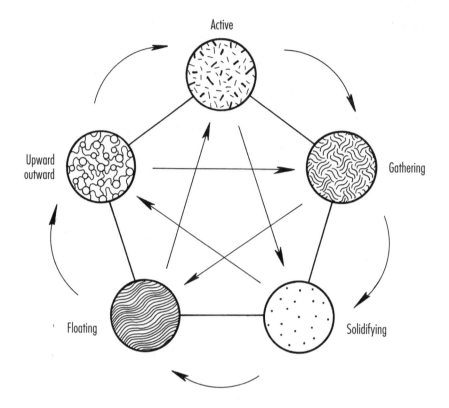

Active

Gathering

Solidifying

Floating

Upward
outward

Five Energies Going

black in a room will diminish physical energy quickly and can cause a lack of clarity; just the right amount can lead occupants to greater precision. In the psyche, black plays the role of the shadow figure, the character hidden from our conscious, waking thoughts. We have a lot to learn from this part of ourselves, but we can easily be overwhelmed by its projected influence in daily life. The use of black in the design process, like that of other colors, needs to be very carefully considered. Like their element, Water, both blue and black are extremely important to use in appropriate amounts.

Water nourishes the next energy, Wood, which moves *upward and outward.* Wood energy is not "hard" like a tree, but rather is moving similarly to the energy of a tree. It is associated with the early morning, the spring season, and the color *green*. The predominant color of the vegetable kingdom, green signifies growth. Its wavelength stimulates bone growth and good posture. In most cases, green also has a strong healing effect on the liver and gall bladder, stimulating the creation of bile, which is used in the body to emulsify fats in the digestive process. Too much green in a room, other than in plants, can create a naive idealism, its vibration uprooting the occupants, moving them away from grounded realism. Used more delicately, green stimulates possibility, affecting the nervous system much as a parent would affect a child when encouraging them to "go ahead and try." Green is only *becoming* active—moving toward fire, but not yet fully charged.

Wood nourishes the next energy, Fire, which is *pulsating, active* energy. Fire is associated with midday, when the sun is overhead; the summer season, when nature is very active; and the color *red*, the most highly charged wavelength in the visual spectrum. Using the color red in the design process will stimulate activity that, if excessive, may create great difficulty for occupants. The use of red in prisons or mental hospitals, for example, has been shown to create violent behavior, causing residents to become more excitable and experience greater levels of stress. Large, vivid patches of red in curtains, upholstery, or carpeting excite the mind and can contribute to migraines, impatience, and general anxiety. Red is seen infrequently in nature, appearing mostly in times of heightened activity, another indication that red carries a strong charge. The proper use of red can induce passion and sensuality, stimulating the sexual libido. It is no coincidence that certain districts in urban areas are distinguished by a red light.

Physically, red will strongly excite the digestive system, accelerating the process of fermentation in the stomach. Open wounds or sores take longer to heal when exposed to red light, as the blood will take longer to coagulate. As an aid in food preparation, a red cloth draped over bread dough, homemade pickles, or sauerkraut, for example, will accelerate the fermentation process. In the home, parents of young children should be careful not to use too much red in their children's rooms or clothing, as it may overstimulate a small child. In contrast, for more mild, fair-skinned children, it may prove to be quite helpful. Red is like fire: both positive and harmful energies are present. Handle with care!

Fire turns into ash, creating and nourishing the energy of Earth, the *gathering* force of the soil. As the energy moves inward and condenses, Earth brings nature to fruition, as we do at the end of a day. The harvest season, also referred to as the late summer, is the time of Earth and is further associated with the color *yellow,* moving inward. The use of yellow in an environment stimulates occupants to become more aware of the gathering of energies, promoting socialization. The yellow rose, long associated with friendship, can be very soothing if used as an accent rather than the primary part of a floral arrangement.

Less intense than red, yellow can be said to be more inspiring than stimulating, as its wavelengths are more closely attuned to the intellect and society. Much has been written to suggest that yellow was the favorite color of Socrates and Confucius, among many other philosophers. This color motivates individuals to consider their relationship with the masses, drawing introverts out, and reducing the likelihood of introspection. In the West, yellow was rarely used in religious ceremony. The White House landscapers could have a considerable effect on the government were they to plant more yellow flowers around the perimeter of this power center. Its energy would begin to gather a stronger, social force around the president through the vibrations yellow creates.

Finally, Earth hardens over time into the energy known as Metal, the force of *solidification*. Metal is the end of the day, and year, when autumn appears and nature prepares to turn inward. Metal is the culmination of the cycle of transformations of energies and is associated with the color *white*. In healing, there is no purer color available than white, as it is in reality a harmony of all colors and wavelengths. White fabrics, flowers, and clothing suggest purity and refinement, an unfortunate association that probably led to the bleaching of whole-grain flours, which strips them of their nutrients. White bread has artificially added nutrition, necessary after it has been refined. This process, called enriching, is truly one of the most oxymoronic practices of the "civilized" world. The cowboy with the white hat, always the "good guy," is another product of our obsession with purity. The dastardly villain, dressed in black, is instantly associated with evil. Society must work very hard to overcome these deeply rooted stereotypes, as they have trapped us in so much unconscious, prejudiced thinking.

The Five Transformations are created by a *cycle of creativity*, or nourishment, moving clockwise through the five phases. Each energy is dependent upon the one preceding it in what is referred to as the parent-child relationship. Water is the parent of Wood, Wood the parent of Fire, and so on. Within the creative cycle is a system of checks and balances called the *control cycle*. In this internal system, each energy controls the child's child, or grandchild, and is controlled by a different energy, the parent's parent.

Water controls Fire; that which is very active must be kept in check by a still hand. One of the many different ways in which we can see the five transformations in life is in anatomy and physiology. In traditional Chinese medicine, the Fire energy of the body is the heart, while the Water is ruled by the kidneys. We know in physiology that it is the kidneys that regulate blood pressure—a demonstration of Water keeping Fire from raging out of control.

Wood controls Earth, the former's upward, outward movement balancing the soil's tendency to gather too much and become hardened. Fire controls Metal through "melting," Earth controls Water by "absorbing," and Metal controls Wood by solidifying energy that may move too strongly up and out. The whole system has brilliant symmetry and serves as a cornerstone of the theoretical structure on which the ancient philosophy from the East is based.

Colors in harmony, like the parent-child relationship, will occur in the cycle of creativity, or nourishing cycle. Red with yellow, for example, conveys a strong, active, gathering energy (as apparently one fast-food chain knows very well). Red alone with white is not nearly as attention getting. Green and red together are powerful, whereas green and yellow conflict somewhat and move our chi up and out and down and in at the same time—and eventually nowhere. Add a splash of red to tie them together, and there is the possibility of more movement. Green controls yellow.

In feng shui, as in nature, the more-intense colors are used sparingly, more as accents, or when consciously creating a certain effect. The center of the spectrum, green, can appear within our homes in the form of plants with only a moderate effect of moving energy upward, symbolizing growth. Too much red in a preschool will cause children to bounce off the walls with hyperactivity, as studies have shown. Violet may pacify an office environment, causing drowsiness, but may be the perfect choice in a room where tranquility is desired. In commercial enterprises where money is the primary concern, violet is as far away from materialization as we can move before we cross the line and become "invisible." Although violet or purple may be the personal preference of a business owner, their use in the interior design of offices is not likely to increase profits. Stronger colors help to manifest things in the material world.

Where a calmer environment is more desirable, as in the bed-

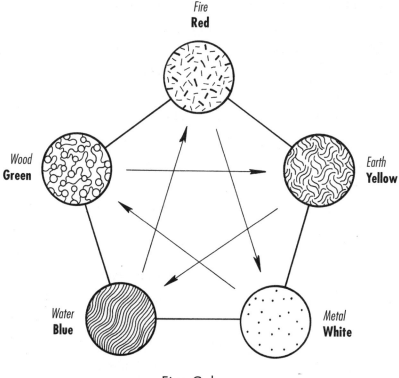

Five Colors

room, large red curtains may contribute to insomnia. If it is just a splash of red in the bedspread, in a few flowers, in a picture or a work of art, this is less likely to occur. Dark shades like gray or black may create depression or neutrality, in either case lacking any real definition unless used in combination with stronger colors. Using gray in schoolrooms or government offices makes these environments very boring.

Quantity Changes Quality

A well-known axiom of the Unifying Principle is important to remember when considering the use of color. Each individual will perceive the vibration produced by color differently. Our physical and emotional states are changing constantly, together with our preferences. As a child, your favorite color, like your best friend, probably changed quite frequently. But it is the *quantity* of any one color that matters—the amount affects the quality of our experience.

Rooms where the overall color scheme is orange or yellow will benefit from a splash of red; however, too much red can overpower an environment, intensifying the vibration. A touch of blue or violet in the same room may have little or no effect; these cool colors must be used more generously to achieve any result.

Intense colors attract our eyes—especially when they are placed in contrast to milder ones. Too much of an intense color, like red or orange, could have the opposite effect. Black can be quite dramatic when used properly; it will be heavy, or even somber, when there is no contrast. In an environment that uses some of almost every color, the eye cannot distinguish one from the other and becomes almost blinded. Each of the five energies has a uniquely different effect and must be used to create a comfortable flow of energy designed to achieve a particular purpose.

> The five colors blind the eye.
> The five tones deafen the ear.
> The five flavors dull the taste.
> Racing and hunting madden the mind.
> Precious things lead one astray.
> Therefore the sage is guided by what he feels
> and not by what he sees.
> He lets go of that and chooses this.
>
> —Lao Tsu

COLOR WORKSHEET

The following practice test is designed to help you better understand the proper use of color in feng shui. Refer to the text in this chapter if you are not sure of the correct answers. Once you have completed the test, you will have a basic understanding of the principles discussed in this section.

1. A woman with a pale yellow loveseat in her living room has decided to purchase two or three small pillows to be placed on it. How would the colors she uses affect the furniture? What colors should she avoid?

2. You have just received a dozen red roses from a secret admirer. Checking your china cabinet, you find no glass vases—only one that is royal blue with black edging and another that is made of creamy white china. Which one do you choose? Why?

3. You work in the sales department of an automobile dealership, and sales are off this month. The boss offers you a choice of two new chairs for your desk to replace the old folding one you have been using—a black leather chair and another covered in forest green fabric. Which one do you choose? Why?

4. The new trendy restaurant that just opened in your neighborhood is decorated with red walls. What kind of energy would you expect to find there? Explain.

5. You are throwing a party to celebrate the merging of your company with a former competitor. Their president's secretary, who has been appointed to coordinate the event with your approval, hands you a list of supplies for the black-tie affair. The tables will be accented with colorful centerpieces. They are open to your suggestions. Any comments?

6. Your daughter has broken her leg while skiing and is in traction, laid up in a hospital. She says she needs a new nightgown to wear—the one the hospital gave her isn't very comfortable. What would be your first color choice?

7. Your children, who spend a lot of time together in the playroom in the basement, always seem to be getting into arguments when they are in this room. What would you look for, and do, in relation to color to change the situation?

8. The copywriters at the advertising agency where you work aren't feeling very inspired these days. Checking his or her open-plan offices, you find a symphony of color everywhere, with no one shade in clear command. Any suggestions?

9. The small powder room off the entry hall has black-and-white checkered tiles on the floor. Your mate asks you to choose some new guest towels to be used there. The local bed-and-bath store has only pale green, bright red, or canary yellow, all with black piping on the edge. Which one would you choose, and why?

ANSWERS

Colors are more than just a matter of personal preference. Your choice of colors, patterns, textures, designs, and materials all affect human behavior in any environment. Though it is not necessarily "right" to choose one color over another, certain colors will help you to achieve harmony and balance, and others will create conflict and discordant energy.

1. Using white on the pale yellow loveseat would create an energy of "settling down." Using red or orange would activate the user more. She should avoid pure green, blue, or purple, as they conflict with white unless there are additional tones to harmonize them.

2. Roses in a royal blue vase may be elegant to some people, but the strong blue will diminish the red of the rose. The flowers will be uplifted (with their intended romantic energy) if placed in a vase made of white china.

3. Black, the absence of color, diminishes energy. A green chair will get you up and out, encouraging a rising energy.

4. Red walls in a dining area activate chi—sometimes too much. Although there may be a lively, talkative crowd in the restaurant, excessive energy in a dining area may be counterproductive to healthy eating. Red overstimulates the appetite and more stomach acid is produced.

5. Look to see what the new corporate color scheme will be and display it prominently. If there is an opportunity to use yellow flowers, the energy of gathering earth, it will help support the merger.

6. Green will help her bones to heal more quickly. Avoid blue or purple when structural problems are present.

7. Too much red or orange or vibrant "neon" colors in a play-room can cause hyperactivity. (Cutting chi might also be present.)

8. Creative energy is flowing in an ad agency and needs curved lines, like brushstrokes of color, to support it. Try to harmonize the area with blues and greens, like streams of water and growing plants, with only the occasional splash of vibrant colors. Reduce blacks, grays, and washed-out colors.

9. Pale green is a quiet color, and may make a small powder room seem peaceful but dull. Red is "classic" in this combination, and could make the room feel very elegant. Yellow is the weakest choice, as there is the least contrast for balance.

But the right answer—the only answer for all of these—is to choose the color you feel is the best because you say so!

Chapter 13

When the Magic Works

Inch by inch, row by row, gotta make our garden grow,
All it takes is a rake and a hoe, and a piece of fertile ground.
DAVE MALLET

Take It Slow

As you change your perceptions of the world around you through feng shui, more and more of what you already know begins to be confirmed by your experience. Belief is replaced by certainty, doubt by possibility. The magic can happen so quickly that it may be difficult not to get carried away by the immensity of what using feng shui could mean in other parts of your life.

Sharing the Secret

There is an old story about Mahatma Gandhi, whose courage, common sense, and inspiring view of the world affected millions of people. One day, a mother brought her young son to meet the wise old man. "Kind sir," she began, "my son will not stop eating candy. He is ruining his appetite and his health. Because he knows of your wisdom, would you please tell him to stop?" Gandhi quickly replied, "Please come back and see me in two weeks." The startled mother took her son and left and, as instructed, returned two weeks later. Gandhi smiled upon seeing them again and, kneeling down, looked right into the little boy's eyes. "Young man, please do as your mother asks. All these sweet things cannot help you to be strong and healthy." Gandhi rose and stood proudly before them both. Bewildered, the mother asked, "Why did you have us return after two weeks? That is what I wanted you to tell him then—I don't understand." "Two weeks ago," he replied, "I had not stopped eating candy myself!"

Beyond just practicing what you preach, using feng shui in your life will give you a greater appreciation and respect for other people's lives. If you really want others to benefit as you have, you are likely to have a far greater influence as an example of positive change than as another proponent of an unheard-of system.

Improving on a Good Thing

Instead of racing through your environment seeking to cure all ills, continue by going further with what you have created. Clear *more* clutter from Earth *after* a new mate shows up. *Repot* that old plant you moved into Heaven to expand further your new relationship with a supportive friend. *Maintain* the sparkling crystal you placed in Wind, even though the blessings are already flowing, by keeping it spotlessly clean.

Also, look at both bigger and smaller baguas, and make other changes in the same house of the bagua but in different settings. For example, if you got a new job after clearing the clutter and placing a cure in Water in your house, look for the Water area in your new office, find it in your bedroom, and locate the spot on your plot that correlates with this energy. If you do not clear all three of these areas too, or others that carry the influence of Water, the results may be only temporary, like a remedy in medicine that does not treat the cause of sickness but only the symptoms.

You might also begin to ask yourself why Water has been stagnant in relation to your body and health, which you can better understand after using the information on feng shui in the body presented in Chapter 17 and the chapter after that, Feng Shui and Health. What steps can you begin to take from the *inside out* that will further strengthen the new direction your life is taking?

So when positive results begin to be apparent, the most prudent approach is to both broaden and deepen your horizons, expanding into related areas like health and related astrologies and delving deeper into the philosophy of feng shui as it is expressed in the *I Ching*.

A New Reality

If you don't know where yer at,
you can't see where yer goin'.
WILL ROGERS

When you return to the Self-Evaluation Worksheet in Chapter 1 after changes brought about by installing cures have become evident, you will be able to reassess your life and see just what has really happened. Reviewing the affirmations and priorities list from Chapter 4 a month or two after you first created them may seem like reading old notes from your private journal. How you felt about your job, relationships, and life in general is likely to surprise you because the positive changes that begin to occur after practicing feng shui greatly affect your perspective. A story shared by a successful consultant helps to illuminate this point.

Robert was a single professional who loved Harley Davidson motorcycles. He owned two bikes, one with a sidecar for a friend to accompany him on his frequent weekend outings. Robert had all the Harley regalia, and his black leather jacket, key chain, pen and pencil set, cigarette lighter, and T-shirts all carried the official insignia.

Everywhere he went, Robert met others who shared his passion; he encountered Harley aficionados at the post office, theaters, local restaurants, and in the office building where he worked. He attended meets, exhibitions, and weekend outings dedicated to the culture of motorcycling. But most of all, it seemed that everywhere he looked, there were Harleys.

Eventually, Robert fell in love with a woman who shared his passion, and they spent their leisure hours biking into the backcountry in search of life's many adventures. Soon, Robert proposed (while on his bike), she accepted (embracing him from behind), and they were married. Not long after their honeymoon, she announced that she was pregnant and that her doctor had recommended that she curtail her cycling until after the birth. Undaunted, and tremendously happy about the prospect of becoming a father, Robert continued to enjoy the world of Harleys on his own, always the faithful husband and father-to-be. The nursery was soon outfitted with all the basic necessities, and their house and hearts were filled with love. Still, everywhere he went, he saw Harley Davidson motorcycles.

They were blessed with a new son, a future cycle enthusiast to be sure. Shortly after the birth, Robert boarded his bike to spread the news and hand out the traditional cigars. But a funny thing happened. Everywhere he went, at every stop sign and tollbooth, in front of the post office and at work, he noticed *Volvo station wagons.* Strapped in the backseat of every one was a child's car seat. Harley Davidsons totally disappeared from sight, and Volvo station wagons began to pop up like daffodils in the spring. Red ones, black ones, old ones, new ones. To his utter amazement, they were everywhere.

Considering that there'd been no massive recall of motorcycles that month, nor was anyone giving away free Volvo station wagons, Robert realized that the world hadn't really changed at all—*he had changed.* The invisible, subconscious images forming deep in his nervous system told him that his world had now become the world of the family, that transportation needed to be safe, that motorcycles and babies don't mix, that the quiet, reliable protection of a sturdy car—with space for a stroller and diaper bags—was the *new reality*. Harley Davidson bikes disappeared from the world of his unconscious imaging, and in its place was a totally new paradigm. How the world occurred to him, his vision and perspective of everyday life, had been altered by external changes on the physical plane.

When the changes from feng shui begin to occur in your everyday life, you will be creating your own new pattern, different from what was there before; furthermore, this pattern will change the way you see the world—and there is nothing you can do to prevent it. This process is very much like the old children's puzzle in which you are shown a pretty picture of a forest. Somewhere in the trees, there is an owl, a snake, and a butterfly. As you look at the drawing, you see nothing but trees, leaves, and flowers. You cannot believe that these animals are in the picture! "Look very closely," says your friend, or, "Don't try so hard to see them, and they will appear!" Finally, after you stare at it for ten minutes, the owl's shape comes into view—and then you see the snake! A few seconds later, the butterfly shows up on a leaf, sitting right there in the middle of the picture!

What you can no longer do is look at this picture *without* seeing all three animals, although only moments before, you would have been willing to bet good money that they were not even there. Your reality has been changed by the appearance of something unexpected. Soon, you take it for granted, and there is no turning back.

Removing and Moving Cures

Because of the impressions this type of experience makes on our memories, a pattern of experience emerges. Then it becomes very difficult to change these old patterns permanently. After you see how much your life has changed as a result of installing feng shui cures, you may actually want to make the phone *stop* ringing with job offers or suitors and may need to remove a cure. If you do, be certain to have in your mind an appropriate visualization to direct your life toward the way you want it to be.

Don't add clutter to cancel the effect of a cure. Don't try to change your front door in order to "shift" your bagua. You will always have the power to create your own life and reality, and with a little bit of practice, you can adjust the effect of the cures as easily as you turn down the volume on your stereo. Feng shui *evolves,* and with it, your experience will change.

If you should decide to move and are concerned about affecting the cures from which you have already benefited, go slowly. Look at the bagua in your new home or office, and you will be able to easily see what needs to be done. Each space is very different, although the floor plan may be exactly the same. Dimensions, colors, textures, patterns, orientation, and location all affect the internal bagua. Any space you choose will integrate with your life in a slightly different way—on another frequency or another vibrational level. As you become more confident, moving cures in the same environment, like rearranging furniture, will become a good way to improve the flow of vital energy in your space and in your life.

Chapter 14

Our Future:
Feng Shui and Children's
Environments

If we don't stand up for our children,
then we don't stand for much.

Marian Wright Edelman

Some years ago, a family who was planning to move sought out a feng shui consultant to help sell their house that had been on the market for months without a buyer. The owners had taken some classes and read a few books, so they understood how feng shui could positively affect an environment. Shortly after entering the home, the consultant noticed the likely imbalance caused by the angle of the roof of the new house next door. The offending element was easily remedied, resulting in a five-minute consultation.

Determined to get her money's worth, the mom then invited the consultant to her daughter's bedroom. "Is she having trouble sleeping?" he inquired, after observing the mirrors covering folding closet doors. "She has the most terrible nightmares, and she's so withdrawn," her mother replied. The mirrors, positioned parallel to the child's bed, reflected her image as she slept and broke her reflection into sections; when the doors were open, they created a sawtooth pattern.

The consultant then suggested an experiment for two weeks: cover the mirrors with a blind that could be pulled down each night, mounted on the molding above the closet. If her sleep improved, then remove the mirrors and install sliding wooden doors without mirrors.

Next, this determined mother moved to her son's room. There were bright red walls, vibrant carpeting in a "computer chip" motif, and a bed placed so that the boy's back was turned to the door. The headboard was against a wall with numerous electrical cords protruding from it. Recognizing the unsettling energy in such an environment, the consultant commented that this fellow must be "quite a live wire." The mother laughed, a confirmation of what a room like this could create: an occupant who was always in motion and couldn't relax unless exhausted. Again, the design of the bedroom was implicated in a problem that no one had really noticed was related to the room. This time, the consultant suggested that she repaint the walls a cooler color, move his bed, and change the carpet to one without a frenetic pattern.

Months later, the consultant received a lovely note: "My daughter slept soundly the first night we covered the mirrors, and she has become more outgoing. My son slowed down considerably when we toned down his room." These changes came about because a wise parent knew that feng shui plays a key role in the environment where children live, sleep, and play.

Helping Children Grow

While there are certainly other factors that probably contributed to this girl's nightmares and the boy's hyperactivity, the relationship between physical and mental health and the environment is very well established. We spend more than a third of our lives in the bedroom, making it perhaps the most important room in the house. We grow while we sleep, so the environment of a child's bedroom is like the soil around a young seedling. Environmental psychologists and feng shui practitioners have observed similar truths, namely that a bedroom's color, materials, shape, and furniture placement strongly affect the occupant's emotional and physical well-being. It thus makes good sense to bring more awareness into the bedrooms of our children beyond what appears in mainstream interior design or environmental psychology.

Children's rooms need to feel safe, loving, and warm. One of the most pleasant ways to brighten a child's room is to hang a faceted crystal in a window where plenty of sunlight will shine through, refracting colors and dancing rainbows all over. Other crystals and natural minerals can be placed in different ways to add color, enhance chi, and bring a bit of solidity into the space. Encourage the child to keep them clean, as described in Chapter 10.

A child's room is also an important atmosphere where health is nourished through a relationship with the natural world. Younger children benefit immensely from a relationship with various aspects of nature, whether through plants and flowers, photography, posters, and motifs on wallpaper or bedspreads, or by actually bringing in a guinea pig, turtle, or aquarium. Keep them clean and enjoy the new friendships that emerge.

Nine Action Steps to Take Now

Making adjustments to an environment according to basic principles of feng shui can often result in significant behavioral improvements. As with dietary recommendations, each family's concerns are different and must be considered in each individual circumstance. The bedroom is primarily a place for relaxation, not activity. Every parent wants to maximize a child's health and learning abilities, and using feng shui can be a beneficial enhancement. Here are nine things to do right now that make a difference:

1. *Choose cooler colors and limit patterns.* White, blue, green, and beige are good for walls and fabric. Hot colors like red or orange are for accents.

2. *Don't force a certain motif on your child.* Even young children can participate in the design process without losing the basic desire of a parent for one main direction. Age-appropriate choices for posters, sheets, and carpeting will change as a child grows. The Cookie Monster or pictures of giraffes and polar bears may be great choices for a toddler; as the child gets older, one would expect to see these elements replaced.

3. *Use soft, flowing lines.* Square or rectangular nightstands, tables, desks, and dressers are acceptable if their corners are slightly rounded, making for a softer feel. If a room is too linear and rigid, a child can easily become a reflection of the inflexibility of the design.

4. *Make the environment as natural as possible.* Children need to be infused with vitality inside their bodies through the intake of good, healthy food. Surround them with the same considerations and choose natural fibers like cotton, wool, or hemp. For furniture and flooring, use wood, bamboo, etc., and try to avoid synthetic materials or plastic surfaces. More information is available in Chapter 16, "Back to Mother Nature."

5. *Bring nature into the space.* Add small plants, shells, rocks, driftwood, leaves, and flowers to bring nature in. Images of the ocean, fish, rainbows, beautiful sunrises, and the smiling faces of friends and family create the most healthy, natural environments.

6. *Eliminate clutter.* Clutter stagnates the flow of energy. Create a ritual to give away old toys, stuffed animals, and games in order to clear space and help others in need. Imagine a world where less is actually more, and the pure creativity inside every

child comes surging through. And don't do the work by yourself—children should pitch in to help clear the clutter and will feel great when the job is done.

7. *Give children a sense of security.* Younger children especially need to feel that their rooms are safe havens. Place beds in the "control" position, opposite and away from the door, with the head furthest from and in full view of the entrance. A "controlled bed" allows for maximum control and feelings of protection. While deadbolts and smoke detectors may help create a sense of security should an emergency arise, subtle placements do more to put a child at ease in the bedroom.

8. *Minimize electricity in a child's bedroom.* Electrical currents can interfere with sleep. Unless absolutely necessary, avoid nightlights or add motion detectors to them to illuminate a path to the toilet should the need arise. Total darkness allows for the body's melatonin to be properly distributed through the body, enhancing the quality of relaxing sleep. If building a child's bedroom, try not to run the electrical wires behind the headboard. If they are already installed and you suspect they are not well shielded, cover the wall with a natural material like corkboard—the perfect bulletin board surface for all those postcards, photos, posters, autographs, and certificates of achievement!

9. *Carefully consider how much light, reflection, and space—and what type—is needed.* Combine general and task lighting with natural light. Cover bare bulbs with shades or install indirect-lighting fixtures. Place mirrors where they reflect light from a window and give children another "opening" for more space. Mirrors should never reflect children in bed; reflections drain energy during sleep instead of restoring it.

A child of five would understand this.
Send someone to fetch a child of five.

GROUCHO MARX

As children learn more about feng shui instinctually, don't be surprised if they make some suggestions to their friends. If you remain flexible, feng shui can be a fun, joyful, and collaborative way for you and your children to improve family life and bring harmony into the home. We are never too old and never too young to play, play, play.

Chapter 15

Feng Shui at Work

I am too smart of a businessman to ignore something that has been around for three thousand years.

BILLIONAIRE INDUSTRIALIST

The Changing Workplace

There are now hundreds of inspiring books and innovative seminars and workshops aimed at changing the way we conduct business. Corporations and nonprofit organizations are clamoring for new ways to sell their products and services; management and labor, strongly influenced by the emerging powerhouses of their Asian competitors, are rewriting contracts, discarding old labor systems, and reinventing the workplace. Catalog sales and money-back guarantees empower consumers, while in-house health centers, concern for work-related stress, and sensitivity training improve worker efficiency and job satisfaction. Over the last few years, change has come so quickly that a company's success depends most of all on moving away from "business as usual." In nearly every industry, information equals power, and innovation spells profit.

One unfortunate effect of this massive shift can be seen in how far away many work environments have moved from the natural world. Buildings with windows that do not open provide "fresh air" through high-tech ventilation systems. Computer workstations surround employees with pulsing electromagnetic charges. Cell phones held inches away from brains receive ultrahigh waves, strongly affecting the nervous system. Plastic plants adorn lobbies that have artificial lighting. Copy machines, furniture, and building materials emit toxic gases that slowly erode health. And late shifts, overtime, and sales quotas disrupt the natural rhythms of the internal clock.

There *are* ways to reduce these unnatural forces and neutralize their debilitating effects. In some countries, legislation has brought about a few changes, such as installation of radiation screens on computer terminals or limitations on overtime in high-stress jobs. But even these changes came about long after most people's common sense told them they were necessary. It took years-long studies and political pressure to get the job done.

New disciplines like *baubiologie* that examine geopathic stress, "sick building syndrome," and other environmentally caused illnesses are currently emerging and deserve our attention. Research in such fields can help people interested in these important phenomena learn how to improve the workplace. In addition, you can use the principles discussed in this book to make your work environment a more healthy and harmonious space, benefiting others who work with you too. Become even more familiar with the way feng shui relates to our ecology by reading the chapter that follows, "Back to Mother Nature."

When all the trees have been cut down, when all the animals have been hunted, when all the waters are polluted, when all the air is unsafe to breathe, only then will you discover you cannot eat money.

CREE PROPHECY

212

What You Can Do

After your next weekend break or holiday away from the place where you work, go in on Monday morning with a copy of the First Impressions Worksheet from Chapter 6. In the same way you evaluated your home—from a place of "emptiness"—fill in the worksheet for your office, store, or workplace. Also, if possible, ask a few friends to do the same thing, as you did for your house. Then step back from the process and take an objective look at the results. Could you detect a marked difference in noise levels? Were you (or your friends) aware of any unusual vibrations, such as those caused by spinning computer hard drives, cycling air conditioning, or humming electrical machinery? Did you sense any change in air quality? Are there other aspects of the environment that appear to be unhealthy? Simply becoming aware of what you may have been taking for granted all this time is the first important step.

Next, create a bagua grid for your office, plant, or shop, and notice where the houses fall. Determine the negative space and projections, and see how existing circumstances may be influenced by either of these. Look at the wall colors, desk shapes, and artwork. Is there too much warming energy? Is there cutting chi? Do the images and symbols in photographs or graphics depict what you want to create there? Discuss with a coworker a little of what you have learned from changes in your own house, and see if you can come up with suggestions that you might offer your employer or office manager. It may be necessary for you to buy the full-spectrum light bulb or new plant for the office if your boss is not interested or there's "no money in the budget." Considering you spend a quarter of your life in this environment, it will prove well worth the cost and effort to make these positive changes. In many ways, the place you work may be as important as your bedroom.

Your Personal Space

Offices are meeting, gathering, and working areas, reflecting the energies of earth and metal in the Five Transformations. To assure an even and balanced sense of energy in your work environment, first make certain that the lighting in the whole office feels harmonious. Use task lighting for individual areas, but be sure that the room does not look like a space full of spotlights.

Get your desk or workstation in order, remove clutter, and organize your files. Your desk will be a reflection of your brain and intestines. Move the waste bin out of Wind.

Filing cabinets and other organizing systems that are more horizontal than vertical are more appropriate when there is a feeling of too much work. Stacks of letter trays in an office can make you feel that the piles of work are endless. Take that pile of papers and other junk that's been sitting in Fortunate Blessings and put it in order. In its place, put a beautiful crystal, a vase of flowers, or a new plant. Make Earth appropriate for Relationships. A favorite photograph or beautiful object is a better choice than unanswered correspondence or overdue invoices. Go through every area of the bagua and consciously choose what you want to go where, adding cures wherever you feel they are needed. Remember to follow the guidelines on how best to install effective cures.

The shape of your office will foretell the nature of the work supported within. Square offices, or those in rectangles slightly longer than a perfect square, will often make the most money. Irregular shapes, like L's or overlong rectangles with corridors or extensions, make an environment where completing projects is more difficult. Triangular offices, or the use of triangular or diamond patterns on furnishings or carpeting, create conflict and reduce cash.

Ceilings in management offices should be higher than those in support offices nearby—not the other way around. Do not hang light fixtures, plants, mobiles, or other objects directly over desks. Skylights over desks, unless they are very high overhead, disperse energy in the work environment.

Placing the Desk

The ideal placement for a desk is opposite and furthest away from the door. Ideally, a solid wall rather than an open window should back up a desk. If possible, create a space where energy can gather; in the best of circumstances, this area should be the house of Wind, Fortunate Blessings.

The desk should be placed parallel to the wall rather than at an angle, which would create a feeling of conflict in the room. The popular "new age" adjustment to place desks (and beds) at an angle creates problems more often than solutions. Desks should also not be placed too close to the corner, which could create a feeling of limitation. Like a bed, it should never be placed in front of a mirror (you will have twice as much work)!

There should be no common passageway behind an executive's desk, nor should there be any strong artwork placed on the wall behind the desk, as it will distract visitors. Strong artwork, calendars, photographs, diplomas, and other wall hangings may be placed on either side of a desk or in any other area of the office.

Desk Size, Shape, and Surface

Your desk should be large enough to allow both a work surface and available storage area and small enough so that everything is easily within reach. A desk that is very large may be impressive but can easily reduce your efficiency. A desk that is too small can lead to frustration.

Square or rectangular desks, or those with right angles and sharp edges, are more appropriate for commercial enterprises where *making money* is the first priority. Curved, oval, or round desks are better suited for environments where *creativity* is the first priority. When both material success and creativity are of equal importance, choose a desk that combines graceful lines with defined, square edges, being careful not to create cutting chi with the corners. The corners can be rounded.

The surface of your desk should not be too strongly reflective, as it will quickly create eye problems and fatigue. Black desks or desks of other colors that create high contrast will slow you down. You should be able to see "into" your work—it should neither bounce off the desk nor disappear on the surface. Desks for any purpose should be balanced and symmetrical and convey a feeling of organization and calm.

The Telephone

Aside from the computer, your telephone is probably the most important fixture in your office. The ease of its use depends a great deal upon proper placement. Make certain that cords are well concealed and, in particular, that the coiled line between base and handset does not cross your work surface. When you talk on the phone, try to make certain that your spine stays straight, opening a channel between heaven and earth for clear communication and energy to flow. Cradling the phone on your shoulder bends your neck and spine, accelerating fatigue and blocking chi.

If you use a cordless phone or remote headset, keep the base off your desk, replacing the handset in the unit only when it needs charging at the end of the day. In this way, you can keep a cordless phone handy according to your needs. Portable phones that contain both receiver and transmitter in the handset place you at great risk for excess electromagnetic radiation—its effect on the central nervous system is implicated in suppressed immune function. If you are accustomed to using a cell phone very often, be certain to use protective peripherals and the speakerphone option as much as possible. Constant exposure to cell phones near our heads cannot be healthy—regardless of what the manufactures claim. Don't forget how long it took for tobacco companies to admit the dangers of their products.

Clear the Environment Daily

Fatigue in an office environment often comes from an excess of positive ions in the environment, created primarily from electronic machinery and lack of fresh, circulating air. Aside from the many modern devices available for balancing EMF vibrations to protect office workers, one way you can greatly increase negative ions in your environment is to wipe down the surface of your desk daily with plain water. Doing so every time you empty your trash can assure you of a clean, calm, and healthy environment in which to work.

Putting greater attention into relating your office to the bagua and balancing your whole work environment will have a dramatic effect on your creativity and success. Then, sit back and enjoy the ride. Miracles *can* happen!

Chapter 16

Back to Mother Nature: Feng Shui and Ecology

We're in a giant car heading toward a brick
wall and everyone's arguing over where
they're going to sit.
DAVID SUZUKI

No one can live without some awareness of the pressing issues of climate change, environmental degradation, and our critical relationship with the natural world. Ecology is hardly a theme most people associate with feng shui, but few subjects come as close to describing certain aspects of each other's core tenets. Following George Buffon's *Historie Naturelle,* a brilliant thirty-six-volume compendium published in the late 1700s that led to the founding of the field of biogeography, the study of ecology emerged late in the nineteenth century. The subject became more popular during the 1960s, when environmental activists and scientists began to recognize our relationship to nature and the accompanying impact of human behavior. Many early Greek philosophers before the birth of Christ would write extensively on the subject of ecology, but it was Charles Darwin who published the first ecological experiment, in 1816.

Ancient Chinese texts on our relationship with nature abound with great wisdom about so many essential subjects; any so-called "ecologist" or feng shui practitioner must read at least a few. Topics as simple as garden design and as profound as an examination of ecofeminism can be found in literature written centuries before the

Christian era. These works need to become part of the overall conversation that includes vital design approaches like feng shui; it is for this reason that ecology is addressed here.

It is a wholesome and necessary thing for us to turn
again to the earth and in the contemplation of her
beauties to know of wonder and humility.
RACHEL CARSON

Should those of us who practice feng shui take on a more active role in society to promote environmental awareness? Not to do so would be to live detached from others in the community, entirely oxymoronic to the adage "man and soil not two." When the pesticides we use on our lawns damage the health of our neighbors, we cannot sit idly by and be content with our healthy looking, green grass.

Everything "green" is red hot. Green residences, green hotels, and green materials are all in vogue, thanks in great measure to a shift in consciousness as we consider not only the negative consequences of living in a toxic environment but also the immense benefit on many levels of complying with the principles of ecological sustainability. Urban design projects now flourish in every corner of the globe; indeed, in some cases legislation like those outlawing plastic bags or harmful contaminants are forcing us to face the music. Feng shui plays a vital role in exploring these issues because of its core principle of respect for our environment and its understanding of our place in nature.

Over the last two decades, numerous works have zeroed in on these issues in great depth; moreover, dozens of conferences and scholarly seminars have been convened, affording an opportunity not just for the one-sided narrative of a text but also for many provocative and spirited exchanges between academics, environmental activists, philosophers, and ordinary citizens.

More and more, feng shui enthusiasts are evident at these gatherings, as their own sensibilities and understanding of the natural world make invaluable contributions. All seem to share essentially the same goal: to declare that the environmental crisis is a spiritual issue first and foremost. Significant indictments against the Catholic church for its failure to take an active role in the environmental arena have sparked a raging debate.

Sustainability

Ecologists today can be thankful for pioneers who recognized that the model for the design of homes and the use of land was best found in Mother Nature herself. Although iconic architect and Oxford scholar Christopher Alexander tried to make the case in *A Pattern Language* (1977) and *A Timeless Way of Building* (1979), he found it imperative to further develop his basic thesis again in *The Nature of Order* in 2004.

In the mid-1960s, many naturalists held seminars in living rooms and church meeting rooms for small groups of activist students interested in learning more about environmental issues. It was in this environment that the first Earth Day was born, and seeds were planted for what would become a burgeoning movement of exploring sustainable lifestyles in harmony with the natural world.

Biologist John Todd earned his doctorate after conducting a study based on the hypothesis that sensory organs worked in the way our intellect might to maintain social order. When the fish he was studying were exposed to pollutants like DDT, their ability to send sensory signals to each other seemed to become severely compromised, unraveling the community and causing a massive disturbance in homeostasis. Parents ate their offspring, and aggressive behavior broke down previously friendly schools of fish. Todd surmised that such pollutants would eventually have the same effects on human beings, so preventing such outcomes became his call to arms.

Might it be that the toxic effects of so many environmental pollutants present in our homes, schools, and public spaces are at least in part responsible for our own aggressive behaviors and the breakdown of community coalitions? Todd was onto something profound that would not become evident for decades—that the materials, fabrics, and design elements we bring into our homes may be causing us harm. The goal of his work was no small aspiration: to transform society through the restoration of natural balance. Alchemy promised to be the perfect metaphor, as it stood for transformation, purification, and redemption of material substance, and in 1970 the New Alchemy Institute in Massachusetts was born.

Following a long-term study on self-sufficiency models, Todd and his colleagues explored solar algae farming using a vital source of minerals and proteins that we presently obtain through expensive products like spirulina and blue-green algae—both available in natural food stores at inflated prices. Sadly for the New Alchemists, the National Science Foundation support for their solar aquaculture project was withdrawn after a short but successful experiment, and they chose not to pursue the work further, instead focusing their energies on environmental issues, farming, and pollution. In hindsight, Todd's aquaculture research turned out to be an important foundation of environmental design, particularly because of its emphasis on human behavior. Ways in which human beings interact with the environment demonstrated a profound awareness of place and a deep commitment to belonging to earth—a modern expression of *shin do fu ji.*

E.F. Schumacher, author of *Small Is Beautiful,* was one of the first philosophers to promote integrated design practices that would eventually lead to new standards for residential and commercial projects, sustainable architecture, and far-reaching design standards. New approaches to waste management, renewable energy, and technological advances are no longer merely an alternative; all of these efforts are finally front and center, and require thorough study in any credible project that employs feng shui to improve our relationships with the environment.

There are undeniable roots of this reorientation in Chinese history. The great sage Confucius spoke frequently about two major themes. The first was "oneness," the interconnectedness of man and nature. Confucius very matter-of-factly insisted that we are very much at home in nature, suggesting that it is there that we find not only delight and comfort but also ethical inspiration. In much of what they did in creating shelter and community, the early Chinese used feng shui to harmonize with patterns and processes of nature—as close to environmental responsibility as any modern-day activist could ever hope for. That these simple truths were abandoned as a result of the industrial revolution is abundantly clear when we trace back the beginning of the degradation of the environment to its onset. Like factory farming and agribusiness, house building and interior design became less about health and wellness and more about profit and unconscious harm. Food preservatives and pesticides used on crops had their counterparts in the formaldehydes and toxic resins of carpeting, paints, and furniture. One must wonder if feng shui can really make any long-lasting improvement to the lives of those who live in polluted residences.

Confucius also wrote about metaphysical anthropocentrism, an approach that assigns the responsibility and the prerogative to every individual. He placed great value on the interdependence of all aspects of nature, seeking to balance and harmonize as we act as both users and caretakers of the natural world from which we gain both sustenance and pleasure. Moreover, this gives us a responsibility to act as stewards of the earth much in the same way American Indians or early naturalists suggest. Practiced in this manner, feng shui could be as much an aspect of the land-ethic environmental theory introduced by American conservationist and philosopher Aldo Leopold as any other modern environmental science.

CASE HISTORY

The Problem: While studying different approaches to natural agriculture, landscaping, and biodynamic farming to bring new life to a tired, overgrown plot of land, one group of students in New England realized they had a problem. They needed to correct the unstable plot plan of a community garden where the Wind corner, symbolizing Fortunate Blessings, was missing. To correct this negative space inside the home, an occupant could use a mirror, crystal, or other cure discussed in Chapter 10; outside the home, a birdfeeder or light would correct this imbalance. In this case, the area was much larger and needed a more substantial installation that would activate the chi along the property line and make a bigger contribution to the neighborhood.

The Solution: One member of the group introduced the idea of Intuitive Feng Shui, and the group came up with a most effective way to solve the problem: put beehives in the area adjacent to the missing corner.

The Result: The commotion and "buzz" of the honeybees activated the chi, pollinating the surrounding flowers (without regard to property lines) and provided measurable value (honey to sell) to the cooperative. The garden produced a plentiful supply of vegetables, herbs, and flowers as the honeybee population grew larger with each season.

Feng Shui: The Holistic Approach

It is when we embrace a sense of the basic order of the universe in which we all participate as generators of life and creation that a holistic sense of feng shui can emerge. Chinese visions of nature insisted that everything in the entire cosmos fit into one organic whole, interacting as equal participants in one constantly changing life process. This order in the universe is the unifying principle employed by the Intuitive Feng Shui practitioner and relates to nature with respectful humility and a reverence for the living earth.

Students of Confucius want the world to change for the better and are willing to become more actively involved with greater responsibility in making that happen; on the other hand, Taoists are content with the way things are, trusting that everything is the way it is for a reason. Like the platforms of opposing political parties, it's clear that many people can possess both views, but to do so, one may need to be content with the way things are and accept "what is" before getting involved to make big changes. The basic tenets of Confucian thought are in reality quite close to environmental activism. In contrast, the Taoist embraces natural spontaneity and a constantly changing reality in nature that, if followed with a dash of Confucianism, would easily lead one to an ethical way of life.

Nine Action Steps to Take Now

Walking our talk means taking action, not just pontificating about the environment and waiting for someone else to come along and fix the problem. Each of us has an opportunity to change many things in daily life that make small but meaningful contributions to harmony and balance in our homes.

Here are nine steps you can take to bring an ecological awareness into fruition:

1. *Avoid plastics and chemicals (Water).* Advertisers and chemical companies had us believing that plastic is a lifesaver when the opposite appears to be true. Consuming water from plastic bottles is now an undeniably toxic practice—not only for the earth but also for us. Beyond the overwhelming pollution the use of plastic bottles has created, evidence now shows that harmful toxins leach into our foods and beverages. For a myriad of reasons, switch to glass—and if you can hold onto and reuse your personal water bottle, buy a good stainless steel portable bottle and take it with you to work, the gym, or anywhere you go. And at the grocery store, don't just choose paper over plastic—bring your own reusable bag.

   Replace unnecessary plastic that cannot be recycled safely with steel, wood, or ceramic alternatives. Do you really need plastic placemats when cotton ones look and feel so much better? How about those kitchen utensils like spoons or spatulas? Countertops? Office supplies? Plastic lurks everywhere in our homes and offices, but there are reliable alternatives. The positive impact when making these changes to our internal and external environment is immediate. Find an earth-friendly dry cleaner, for example, and change polyester fabrics and synthetic clothing and materials to natural fibers.

2. *Buy local and organic (Earth).* The most natural foods to eat are the ones that can or do grow in our own climates. Nature put them there to support us. Eating bananas in very cold regions may make sense from a sensory or nutritional perspective but fail the test of environmental awareness and sensibility.

Foods that grow in the tropics cool us, so enjoy those bananas in the summer if you live in a more temperate climate. Foods grown in the same climatic conditions in which we live match our vibration; furthermore, it makes good ecological sense to shop locally. And who needs the glut of chemicals, pesticides, and preservatives when we can find organic staples for most of what we need to flourish and maintain a healthy body and mind?

Organic sources of whole grains, beans, legumes, flours, nuts, seeds, land and sea vegetables, oils, condiments, fruits, sweeteners, herbs and spices can be easily secured in most major cities. Local farmers markets, food cooperatives, and small roadside stands are wonderful suppliers.

3. *Place plants in and around your home (Thunder)*. The upward, outward energy of healthy green plants throughout our homes lifts chi, brightens spirits, and brings us closer to nature. While it's nice to have small ornamental plants like orchids or lilacs, taller shrubs and houseplants produce greater amounts of the energies we need. Larger environments can tolerate more spiked-leaf varieties, but in general choose plants with more rounded, succulent leaves and blossoms.

An old Chinese proverb suggests that the best time to plant a tree was twenty years ago, and the next best time is today. Beautiful landscaping, especially of the edible variety, not only improves property values but also adds more oxygen and negative ions to the environment where we live and play. Even a couple of potted plants on an urban patio or front porch can harmonize and soothe the spirit of residents and visitors alike. Consider using alternative materials like bamboo, a wonderfully renewable, eco-friendly grass that uses no pesticides and reduces rainforest deforestation.

4. *Compost and recycle (Wind)*. Our fortunate blessings are those things that seem to present problems but can be transformed into assets; therefore, nowhere is this more valid than when thinking about trash. Today, a kitchen plan without incorporating areas for recycling and composting is outdated and not earth-friendly. Composting table scraps can create rich nutrients for the backyard garden, whether you are growing your own organic vegetables or prizewinning begonias. And reducing the amount of waste we send to landfills is the perfect way to tell Mother Earth how much we love her.

Traditional cultures shake in horror when observing the modern practices that have led to so much pollution and harm to the earth and soil. While these practices do take a bit more effort, a shift in perspective in everyday life, the payback—becoming a part of the solution rather than part of the problem—is palpable. Feeling good from the inside about how we live in the world can do more than a boxful of perfect crystals.

5. *Eat whole foods (Tai Chi)*. No single act brings us closer to the earth and more in touch with our environment than changing our blood quality. Because we are what we eat, this means including more whole cereal grains and fresh vegetables in our daily diets and switching to more plant-based proteins and natural, local, and seasonal foods. Chapter 17, "Infinite Connections," tells you more about making the change.

6. *Get to know your neighbors (Heaven)*. Right next door and across the street, you just might find what you're looking for. Asking for help and becoming a helpful friend is not unlike charity: it begins at home. Strong individuals create strong families, and strong families make stronger communities by allying with neighbors to create collectives, buying clubs, bartering groups,

and coalitions too numerous to mention—all part of a "small is beautiful," eco-friendly way of life.

Whether you are young or old, rich or poor, find the common unity we all share with those whose lives are within our senses: the very people we see, hear, and touch every day are part of our world, affording everyone an opportunity to realize our dreams for health and happiness.

7. *Tell the children (Lake).* The long view of ecology means that future generations inherit what we do today. Discussing your choices with children informs and educates. Most schools cover these subjects only peripherally, yet children almost always enjoy learning more about the natural environment. Explain why recycling, new food choices, and natural fibers, for example, are important to you.

To the surprise of many parents, it is the children who lead the way. Children helped launch recycling initiatives, seat belt campaigns, and antismoking efforts, so it is only natural that children will care as much—and sometimes even more—about their own future as their elders. Include them in the conversation every step of the way, and be prepared to do even more when they become more fully engaged.

8. *Deep ecology (Mountain).* Just as environmental concerns are not limited to pollution or climate change, ecology is not just about organisms, bacteria, and the visible environment. Another fundamental study, spiritual or "deep ecology," parallels the more common environmental science approach with which most people are familiar. A term first introduced by the late Norwegian philosopher Arne Næss, deep ecology is a philosophy of profound contemplation over man's interrelatedness to everything in the environment.

With an understanding and study of deep ecology, practitioners of feng shui can do much more than place furniture and crystals, taking on a role for an even larger, more conscious environmental responsibility, and ecological awareness and interdependency. Doing so leads individuals to a deeper awareness of the inner and outer worlds and a living ecology.

9. *What's inside matters most (Fire)*. Every individual controls his or her own chi first and has more power over life than a partner, bedroom furnishings, front doors, or floor plans. Fire is "light giving," the second daughter in Chinese philosophy, an attribute ascribed to this trigram by Fu Hsi. Mankind's destructive rampage of nature requires a fundamental change in the way a society relates to women.

Honoring the work of Kenyan ecologist Wangari Maathai, who pioneered a movement to plant trees throughout her native Kenya, it is clear that women's place in the environmental movement is most justifiably center stage. "Mother" Earth didn't get her name by accident. We need to learn from the profound sensitivities women bring to the ecological movement, to look back at women's contributions in traditional societies and how patriarchal attitudes have resulted in the erosion of our most important values of dignity, respect, and honor for all life.

Chapter 17

Infinite Connections

The body says what words cannot.
MARTHA GRAHAM

Feng Shui in the Body

It is possible to see another manifestation of the bagua and the trigrams of the *I Ching* when looking at the human body. As a trained physiognomist knows well, "the face never lies," and it is here that the bagua appears most clearly.

Because we are not separate from our environment, faces and houses are closely related. The Front Door to the face is the mouth; this means that it occupies the Water position. The house of Fire, symbolizing Illumination or Enlightenment, encompasses the area of the pineal gland, also known as the third eye. Each of the remaining houses is now easy to locate, and the bagua takes on new meaning as an expression of our lives.

Many other symbols of the eight trigrams can be included when we personalize the bagua by using it to look at our faces. For example, darkness around the mouth, indicating stagnation in Water, reveals the beginning of problems on The Journey, our paths in life. Blemishes in Thunder or Lake are a sign of clutter that will be present simultaneously in these same areas in our homes and in our lives. To the experienced eye, the face reveals through feng shui as much about a person's destiny as a good floor plan or photograph of the house.

The whole human body is also a reflection of the bagua. Problems with any part will appear both in the places where we live and work and in the events of our daily lives. A deeper study of traditional Chinese medicine and the trigrams as symbols in the body reveals the inescapable connections we have with our environments.

Differences Between Man and Woman

In one way, gender determines destiny. As a result of who we are biologically, a man will never give birth to a child, nor will a woman manufacture sperm. The Universal Opposites of Heaven and Earth, called yang and yin, symbolize the energies of Man and Woman. The trigram for Heaven is composed of three unbroken lines (all yang); the trigram for Earth is made up of three broken lines (all yin). Yin and yang are always relative terms—one is not superior to the other.

The shape of a house is like the genetic marker of sex. However we may dress or whatever our sexual orientations, underneath it all is a biological distinction that exists even before birth. We may add lilacs and lace to a house whose shape creates a greater yang charge, but the *structure* still carries a predominant energy.

When either of the primary yang (Heaven) or yin (Earth) houses is missing from the bagua inside your home or workplace, creating negative space, it will be difficult for the gender whose house is absent to feel settled there for a long period. Naturally, this effect will vary among individuals, some men having developed more of their feminine, receptive nature and some women having developed more of their masculine, assertive energy.

These symbols carry other charges beyond simple personality traits. The Destiny Chart that follows expands upon the energies that are present in the bagua as they relate to the trigrams. They can be seen as complementary antagonisms for the following aspects.

Destiny Chart

Yang	Yin
Material	Spiritual
The Self	Selflessness
Physical	Mental
Logic	Intuition

A house in which there is a projection in Heaven or Earth or in the two trigrams directly opposite this complementary pair, Wind and Mountain, will embody exaggerated energies of yang or yin, respectively. When it appears as if the house shape also carries a charge of negative space, the correlated energies of yin and yang, as listed in the Destiny Chart, will be missing.

Special care should be taken when considering a house or office of an extremely unusual, unbalanced shape. Although the effect of negative space can be reduced, it is nearly impossible to erase it entirely.

In the figure below, the houses of Wind and Heaven are projections, accentuating forces of yang related to these energies. In general, men will be happier in this house, and women will find it uncomfortable. Both male and female occupants are more likely to be focused on materialism, the intellect, and developing the self. Paradoxically, when people who live in houses this shape are successful, they will more naturally become Helpful People, charged with Heaven's energy.

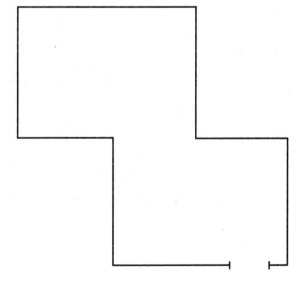

In the following figure, Earth and Mountain can be considered projections, increasing the charge of yin energy. Women will feel more settled here, and most men will feel uncomfortable being here for long periods. This house's occupants are more likely to be aware of their intuition and emotions and to have a spirit of selflessness, not nearly as able to accumulate wealth or material possessions as the occupants of the house in the previous figure. This house creates wisdom through life experience, which will carry more material difficulties but with a greater emotional and spiritual maturity.

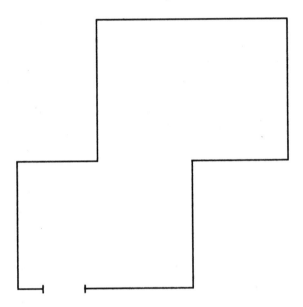

The architecture of Heaven and Earth is perfect in the one house we all must consider: our biological home, the human body. Our true nature, as spirit or energy, lives inside a perfectly ordered and harmonious form. When nourished properly, cleared of clutter, and sensitively supported, the human body heals itself as a result of natural laws—the very same principles that govern the external environment. These principles are the basis of a way of life known as macrobiotics.

What Is Macrobiotics?

Macrobiotics is thought by most people to be a dietary practice that incorporates brown rice, vegetables, and other foods consumed in certain ratios. The majority of those who know little about it believe it to be a diet that is restrictive, bland, and even dangerous, practiced by food extremists without regard to modern science.

Consider the possibility that most of what you think you know about macrobiotics is really just a jumble of mixed impressions. Imagine that you have opened a box containing 237 pieces from thirteen jigsaw puzzles, each needing 100 pieces to complete a whole picture. Most of every puzzle would be unfinished, and you'd more than likely have only a faint idea of what any of them looked like.

Macrobiotics is not a diet at all, but a way of life and an extraordinary philosophy of self-development based on timeless principles of *change* and *choice*. By gradually introducing certain simple foods, exercises, and practices into your everyday life, you begin to bring into focus a harmony and order that is already present. To be aware of this order, you really need not give up anything at all, unless you choose to, but it is clear from years of practice by millions of people throughout the world that consumption of whole, natural foods allows you to have a greater role in guiding your own life.

No foods are forbidden except when your body tells you so.
LIMA OHSAWA, *MACROBIOTIC CUISINE*

Whole cereal grains, like brown rice, corn, oats, wheat, and barley, and whole-grain products, like breads, pancakes, crackers, pastas, and puddings, have been the staple foods of most cultures through-out the centuries.

In ancient Greece the word *macrobios* was used to mean the art of achieving health and longevity through living in harmony with the environment. In modern times, the term was recovered by the Japanese philosopher Georges Ohsawa to represent the healthy way of life, reflecting the spirit of how a healthy person views life: *macro,* meaning "large or great," and *bios,* meaning "life." More specifically, with proper diet we can experience a great life, full of adventure, freedom, and creativity. Ohsawa spent the better part of his life spreading macrobiotic philosophy and dietary reform throughout the world. Since his death in the mid-1960s, hundreds of his friends and students—many of them now highly respected teachers in their own right—have carried on his work.

The macrobiotic approach is one that takes into account the evo-lution of humanity, our relation to the environment, and our indi-vidual needs. The dietary guidelines are not only preventive, aiming to maintain good health and to decrease the incidence of sickness, but can also be used therapeutically by those who are already ill and wish to use natural means of healing.

Although the principles of macrobiotic eating are longstanding practices in many traditional cultures, the philosophical basis of mac-robiotics is the study of change—namely, the principles of relativity, or yin and yang, the basis of all Eastern philosophies, cultures, arts, and medicine.

The Unifying Principle

By observing our day-to-day thoughts and activities, we can easily see that everything is in motion, or in other words, everything changes; electrons spin around a central nucleus in the atom; the earth rotates on its axis while orbiting the sun; the solar system is revolving around the galaxy; and the galaxies are moving away from one another with enormous speed. An orderly *pattern* is discernible, however. Day follows night; winter changes to summer and then back to winter again; during the day we stand up and are active, and at night we lie down and rest.

Starting from this basic understanding, we can classify all phenomena into either one or the other of the two categories, yin and yang. However, because these are relative terms, nothing in the world is absolutely yin or absolutely yang; all phenomena possess both in varying degrees. Yin and yang are always changing into each other in a continual cycle, reflected in the change from night to day and winter to summer, from inhaling to exhaling. Contraction, or yang, produces heat, which eventually causes the expansion of yin; expansion produces coldness, which then causes contraction. As a result, vegetation growing in a more yin, or cold, northern climate is usually smaller, while the vegetation in more yang, or hot, climates is usually larger.

Diet and Health

An appreciation of the importance of proper diet for good health has been largely lost in modern times. Among more primitive societies it was well recognized and used as the basis of medicine. Food is our source of being. Through the vegetable kingdom, all the basic forces of life are combined in a form that can be used by the human organism. Sunlight, soil, water, and air are taken in through the medium of the vegetable kingdom. To eat is to take in the whole environment.

The dietary approach of macrobiotics is not to prescribe a specific diet. Because we are all different—live in different environments, have diverse needs, and do different work—individual diets will vary.

Today, hundreds of thousands of people around the world use macrobiotic principles to select and prepare their daily diet and to restore their health and happiness. Dozens of centers all over the world focus on educating people about macrobiotic principles.

Classification of Foods

To develop a balanced diet, it is helpful to classify foods into categories of relative yin and yang. Different factors in the growth and structure of foods can indicate whether a food is predominantly yin or yang. Because all foods have both yin and yang qualities, in classifying foods we must look for the factors that dominate.

Yin Energy	Yang Energy
Growth in a hot climate	Growth in a cold climate
Foods containing water	Foods that are dry
Fruits and leaves	Stems, roots, and seeds
Growth high above the ground	Growth below ground
Hot, aromatic foods	Salty, sour foods

Yin and Yang Growth Cycles

One of the most accurate methods of classification is by the cycle of growth in food plants. During the winter, the climate is very cold (yin); during this time of year the growing energy descends into the root system. Leaves wither and die as the sap descends to the roots and the vitality of the plant becomes more condensed. Plants that are used for food and grown in the late autumn and winter are drier and have a more concentrated quality. They can be kept for a long time without spoiling. These plants are yang. Examples are roots such as carrots, parsnips, turnips, and onions.

During the spring and early summer, many plants' energy ascends and new greens appear as the weather becomes hotter (yang). These plants are more yin in nature. Summer vegetables are more watery and perish quickly. They provide a cooling effect that is needed in warmer months. In late summer, the growing energy has reached its zenith, and the fruits become ripe. They are generally watery and sweet and develop higher above the ground.

This yearly cycle also can be applied to the part of the world in which a food originates. Foods that find their origin in hot, tropical climates where the vegetation is lush and abundant are more yin, while foods that come from colder climates are more yang. We can classify different foods that grow at the same time of year by seeing their general growth pattern. The root system is governed by yang energy, the tendency to descend. The stem and leaves are governed by yin energy. This energy is expressed in the dominant direction of growth.

The Importance of Whole Cereal Grains

The first time I ate organic, whole-grain bread,
I swear it tasted like roofing material.
ROBIN WILLIAMS

As a society, our tastes have changed dramatically over the past few decades. Meat replaced grains and vegetables as central foods, and shelf life was more a consideration than health. When the pendulum began to swing back toward healthy ways of eating, good taste was a secondary concern. Not so long ago, breads and cookies made with whole grains were heavy, thick, and often tasteless at best—good for little more than doorstops. Fortunately, we've come a long way.

For centuries, humanity has looked to cereal grains as the primary food—the pulse of mankind. This is especially true of the great civilizations of the world. The importance of cereal grains in the evolution of humanity cannot be overlooked. Recently, consumption of whole grains has sharply fallen and has been replaced by animal foods, such as dairy and meat, and refined carbohydrates, such as sugar and refined flour. It is now widely recognized that this shift in diet has led to the development of many of the major health problems in our technological civilization.

The cereal grains are unique among our foods; they are both the beginning and the end of the vegetal cycle, combining seed and fruit. It is for these reasons, as well as the cereals' ability to combine well with other vegetables to provide a wholesome diet, that cereals form the most important, central food in the macrobiotic regimen.

Preparing Our Food

The macrobiotic approach to cooking is unique. When ingredients are simple, cooking is the key to producing meals that are nutritious, tasty, and attractive. The cook has the ability to change the quality of the food in many ways. More cooking—the use of pressure, salt, heat, and time—makes the energy of food more concentrated. Quick cooking and little salt preserves the lighter qualities of the food. A good cook controls the health of those for whom he or she cooks by varying the many different cooking styles. It is no wonder that in ancient times the role of cook was honored; with time, let us hope we can restore this deserved respect for those who prepare our daily fare and give us "our daily bread."

Chewing is an important complement to the macrobiotic diet. It can also be thought of as a form of preparation. A meal should be eaten calmly and with gratitude. One of the best ways of expressing this gratitude is by chewing well so that the food can be digested well and used by the body more efficiently.

The Macrobiotic Way

Macrobiotics is really a common sense approach to life. Since diet and environment may very well turn out to be the most important factors in degenerative illness, becoming aware of the healing qualities inherent in everything we eat gives us greater control over our destinies. In light of the incidence of degenerative illness and general poor health that plagues the world, the macrobiotic approach is a sensible alternative to our over-processed and devitalized foods. The return to a diet more in keeping with that of our ancestors is in order if humanity is to regain its health and vitality.

Macrobiotics is, very simply, internal feng shui. You can do nothing more powerful to transform your life than to follow a diet and way of life based upon macrobiotic principles. Balancing the inner bagua through daily food is the real key to the practice of Intuitive Feng Shui. It is true freedom.

Chapter 18

Feng Shui and Health

To keep the body in good health is a duty;
otherwise we shall not be able to keep our mind
strong and clear.

Prince Gautama Siddhartha

Health is perhaps our most treasured possession. Once thought to be as simple as an apple a day, the mere absence of sickness is only a small part of living a healthy life. In feng shui terms, health is the harmonious interconnectedness of all aspects of one's life—not just good blood pressure or maintaining the proper weight. The bagua reflects the eight aspects of health, meeting in the middle, or Tai Chi, where health converges.

Before examining the physical and emotional relationships found in the bagua, a simple review of each of the eight trigrams reveals the importance of every part contributing to a vital, joyous life.

The Eight Trigrams and Health

Water: Following the Tao of our own lives with power and purpose is possible when this primordial energy is in order. Health in Water keeps our true dreams clear.

Earth: Maintaining genuine, loving, and open relationships with others provides us with an opportunity to deepen our roots. Health in Earth comes with laughter, joy, honest reflection, and support.

Thunder: Our parents and elders gave us our lives. Regardless of the circumstances of our childhood and family life, loving respect for them sustains a positive perspective when we face other challenges. Health in Thunder gives us power to rise above any obstacle.

Wind: To experience life itself as a fortunate blessing begins with gratitude for those who made it possible. Health in Wind means penetrating the duality of good and bad or right and wrong and living freely in the moment of each breath.

Heaven: Friendships enrich our experience by allowing us to explore the illusion of seemingly separate lives. It is through our casual acquaintances and lifelong friends that we find the opportunity to give and receive. Health in Heaven allows us to make a difference in the world.

Lake: As parents and creators, we can easily see the reflection of our own imperfections. Health in Lake means spontaneity and free-flowing creativity.

Mountain: The ability to step away from it all and contemplate the meaning of life regenerates us, making way for change and greater clarity. Health in Mountain gives us access to our inner wisdom.

Fire: With humility and grace, health in Fire makes it possible to walk through life with confidence and inner peace unburdened by what other people think of us.

Room for Improvement

Looking at our homes more carefully shows the direct relationship of certain organs to each room. Each room relates to an organ or system in the human body; therefore, attention to placement, order, and overall design directly benefits the organ function.

The Liver and Hormones

Our kitchens are arguably the most important rooms in our homes, for it is here that we make our blood quality and life force from our daily nourishment. While preparing food, we clean away unwanted dirt and fats from vegetables and meats, cutting away and discarding parts that are not digestible and beginning the process of cooking by adding seasonings, oils, salts, and other elements that ready foods for human consumption. This process is very much like the liver, the body's largest and most complex internal organ, which regulates hormones, forms and secretes bile and acids for digestion, stores and processes fats, and eliminates and detoxifies harmful substances, among many other functions.

The ancient Chinese thought of the liver as the chief military strategist and planner in the body, whose orderly function assured balance and harmony in society. Correspondingly, our kitchens should be orderly and clear, with a good setup for efficiency in food preparation.

Anyone with liver problems, including those with any form of jaundice, hepatitis, cirrhosis, obstructions (like gallstones), or liver cancer must place particular emphasis on the kitchen and its design. Because the kitchen is the one place in the home where the organic opposites of fire and water are present, it is important not to place a sink or washbasin directly next to or opposite an oven or stovetop burners. Also present in the kitchen can be extreme cold energy like the refrigerator or freezer. It is with these polarities in mind that the triangular placement of stove, sink, and refrigerator was popularized—a good solution to harmonize these distinctly different energies.

Like a liver flush or cleanse that some practice in the spring, clearing the kitchen of clutter and waste on a regular basis—as well as maintaining both adequate ventilation and cleanliness—helps support healthy liver function.

The energy of the liver is something like that of a tree, so it is correlated with the Wood element, the east (sunrise), beginnings, and new birth; its complementary organ is the gall bladder. These associations suggest that we bring plenty of leafy green vegetables into our kitchens, both for consumption and decoration; furthermore, processed, refined foods that lack life force diminish the liver's vital, upward force and should be minimized or eliminated. Foods that are most harmful for the liver include deep-fried foods, white flour and white sugar, caffeine, cold drinks, and any foods that cool the body, like excessive raw foods, tropical fruits, or vegetables. Because anger is known to upset the liver's balance, the kitchen should be a peaceful environment, and those who prepare food would be wise to maintain a loving energy.

Kitchens that incorporate a variety of natural materials (ceramic, wood, copper, stone, vegetable fibers, bamboo, etc.) support the kinds of creative cooking styles needed to maintain healthy digestion. A diet rich in quality oils, complex carbohydrates, leafy green vegetables, and a touch of sour taste like lemon or vinegar keeps livers (and kitchens) functioning at their optimum level.

The Heart and Circulatory System

The "heart" of many homes is the kitchen, but more generally, this organ is related to the area of our lounge or primary living room. Friends and family circulate in and out of this space, exchanging stories, listening and relaxing, laughing, and loving. Our living rooms can be a place where passions flare, love is expressed, and deep relaxation can occur. Who among us hasn't taken a nap on the living room couch?

The heart, the minister that according to the Chinese excels with insight, understanding, and gentle control, keeps blood moving through our bodies and circulatory systems. It benefits from both strong, pumping action and deep rest, contraction, and expansion. Blood pressure, actually ruled by the kidneys and Water energy, is maintained in the heart, assuring healthy, gradual adjustments reflective of varying exertions.

In the same way, our living rooms benefit from a variety of furnishings, some to sit more vertically while reading or playing a game, and others to lean back or recline in and more deeply relax. An easy chair, a couch, and accessory ottomans or side tables can be arranged in numerous ways to achieve this end. If space is limited, be careful not to clutter the area just to bring variety. Like occlusions in the heart and circulatory system, too much furniture can be harmful to good circulation and relaxation.

In the body, the heart is protected by the ribcage, a harder covering than in the abdomen over the intestines, for example. This suggests why traditional feng shui design practices placed the living room in such a way as to be protected from the front door. Where possible, it is ideal to site the living room far enough from the entry so as not to be seen when one enters the home. If this is not possible, place furniture accordingly and use a mirror to move energy and light into the space between a chair or couch and the doorway. Where columns are placed, make certain they do not block instinctually used pathways; such unconscious placements are often present when an occupant reports a blockage in the heart or circulatory system.

The heart is related to the summer season, the time when nature displays the most color and flourish. Here then is the place in our homes where we can place flowers and artwork, bright fabrics, and more complex patterns; however, in cases where occupants suffer from hypertension, beware not to use too much red, as long

247

wavelengths excite the cells. Even excess joy and excitement can upset the balance of a healthy heart.

Plenty of light and openness are particularly important in our living rooms, allowing the heart to be free, open, and expressive. A heavy heart, burdened with excess fat in the diet, is often correlated with dark, depressing living areas; furthermore, narrow corridors and hallways between rooms in the home can, like narrowing of blood vessels, contribute to high blood pressure.

Corn—shaped like a heart—is often used to strengthen weak hearts and is a good staple to include in the summer months. Tall grasses like chives and scallions are also known to promote heart energy and prevent blood from coagulating unnecessarily. Most of today's degenerative heart problems are preventable and can be avoided by common sense dietary changes that reduce animal fats and proteins as central foods and increase the use of vegetables, complex carbohydrates, and if desired, some fish and seafood. Heart health is keenly connected with the kidney and lungs, although the complementary organ of the heart is the small intestine. Since one of the most vital aspects of this fiery organ is its relationship to the blood and circulation, the heart can also be subtly influenced by a wide variety of easily obtainable medicinal herbs and tonics.

Soft, receptive furnishings with plenty of pillows, cushions, and pliable surfaces should be plentiful in living areas to mitigate the corresponding hardness in the heart and circulatory system as much as possible. High ceilings without heavy beams hanging directly over seating areas also help to assure that this vital organ continues to function well.

The Spleen and Lymphatic System

Few people can point to the spleen in their body; fewer still understand what it does. Ironic indeed when we know that the spleen is related to the dining room, one of everyone's favorite places to be—and we all know what we do there, too!

Whatever place we eat is our dining room; hopefully it is unencumbered by piles of homework, business papers, blaring televisions, or a small project that somehow extended well past the weekend. The dining room is the sacred space in which we convert the outer world into our cells, chewing thoroughly and beginning the most important starting point of digestion—mixing food with the secretions of our salivary glands. So easily distracted from this essential first step, many of us read, talk, or watch the evening news, losing focus on the work (and pleasure) at hand.

The spleen, corresponding with the energy of soil in the Five Elements, filters blood, removing harmful microorganisms, and disposes of old red blood cells. The spleen acts like a chauffeur, carrying blood, lymph, and chi energy throughout the body. It also manufactures antibodies to help us resist infections.

The dining room, and its furnishings and tableware, carry nutrients from the kitchen to the cells via the process of consuming and digesting food. Each transporter—the table, plate, bowl, cup, and utensil, must be clean and free of waste. Similarly, the surface and surrounding area of the dining area is best kept clear of any excess, assuring that the significant role of eating the food we prepare takes place in a harmonious environment.

Ergonomics plays a key role here as much as any other place in our home save the bedroom. Upright posture, made possible by good chair and table height as well as strong, supportive seating, results in our spleen and stomach being properly positioned to receive food in the most ideal way. In contrast, eating while standing up or walking disrupts the normal secretions of digestive juices as well as making it more likely that we will bolt down our food with inadequate chewing.

Saliva carries an essential enzyme called ptyalin, whose role is the breakdown of complex carbohydrates before they go to the stomach, the complementary organ of the spleen. In essence, chewing foods like whole grains is more a matter of mixing than masticating. Fragrant aromas of freshly cooked dishes, tasteful seasonings and condiments, and pleasing presentations in the dining room all combine to stimulate our salivary glands that start the process. Even a lone diner can benefit enormously from setting the table for one, creating an atmosphere for optimum enjoyment and good digestion.

Foods that support the spleen include the whole grain called millet; sweet tastes including those from round vegetables like pumpkins, squashes, and onions; and softer, cooked food like stews and soups with the above ingredients. For those who live in temperate climates, local fall fruits like apples, pears, and sweet berries all support a healthy spleen—and look fabulous in pies or puddings displayed on the dessert tray on the dining room table.

The Lungs and Respiratory System

Most people spend more time in the bedroom than in any other room in the home. We go here to regenerate, to rest the cells, organs, and spirit, slowly releasing tension and accumulated toxins. In the middle of the night, our lungs actually reach their peak of activity, releasing gaseous waste in the form of carbon dioxide. Fresh air and good circulation are key components of a healthy bedroom and maintaining a healthy respiratory system.

The ancient Chinese felt that the lungs and their complement, the large intestines, were responsible for the regulation of the body. Indeed, in that they both process waste (gaseous and solid) and maintain a flowing rhythm when healthy, it is easy to see why they are paired.

In the bedroom, it is the placement of the bed itself that is the most important consideration in feng shui, as described in Chapter 8. Ideally, we should leave the space under our beds open for good air circulation, not unlike the pleural cavity around our lungs; in a similar corollary, a beam crossing the bed will weaken the lungs like a strap tight around the ribcage will prohibit deep inhalations. Beds that are placed directly opposite the door drain energy; beds placed against windows can make it difficult for people to sleep in inclement weather.

Perhaps the most challenging modern appliance in the bedroom is the television. Since the bedroom is a place to sleep and is not a media room, it's best to remove the television altogether and place it in another room. It is simply unhealthy for us to fall asleep with images from the evening news or popular series dancing across our minds. Even the vibration of electrical fixtures around the bed can create electromagnetic imbalances that disrupt and interfere with restful sleep.

Other rooms in our homes can store books, papers, and reading material; don't pile them in the bedroom where the vibrations of thousands of stores, articles, words, and characters fill the space meant for relaxation and renewal; keep reading matter to a minimum if you chose to read in bed. The mix of gases we need for health and vitality, predominantly nitrogen and oxygen, in that order, is not complex; therefore, we need not surround ourselves with a complex mix of other elements in the atmosphere.

The lungs and respiratory system benefit greatly from brown rice, leafy green vegetables like kale and bok choy, and a variety of minerals like those found in the sea and in nuts, seeds, and root vegetables. Spices disperse the energy of the lungs, so for those with lung ailments they are best avoided or minimized. Asthma, an almost exclusively urban disease, is exacerbated by excessive humidity and a lack of helpful intestinal bacteria. It is therefore wise to include fermented foods like sauerkraut, pickles, miso paste, tamari soy sauce, or complements like probiotics to support healthy lung and large intestine function. In the bedroom, this can mean including plants potted in large containers with soils that can hold lots of nourishing humus and peat moss.

Bedrooms are best positioned at the back of the home, farthest away from the front door. This assures privacy, protection, and a restful sleep as well as an atmosphere separate from the hustle and bustle of the kitchen or living areas. Muted colors should be favored in the bedroom, with sparingly applied splashes of vibrant shades. This assures the energy there will not be overly stimulating. Since light prevents the secretion of melatonin, the sleep-inducing hormone, blackout curtains can be very helpful, particularly in urban settings.

The bed itself should be made of natural fibers: latex, cotton, hemp, or other vegetable matter. Box-spring mattresses often interfere with the body's electromagnetic integrity so are best avoided; however, magnetic sleep systems that combine magnetic top mats with far-infrared cotton mattresses and comforters replicate the earth and sun energy we need to restore our cells and help us to rejuvenate muscles and brain function.

Kidneys and Sexual Organs

Finally, Water energy in the home relates to the kidneys and corresponds to the bathroom, a place of purification. Like the organs whose role is to process about fifty gallons of blood to filter out about two quarts of waste products, the bathroom is the place where we cleanse our outer and inner bodies through bathing and the excretion of waste. Complex filters remove waste and release hormones to regulate chemical balances much like when we brush our teeth or scrub our skin with a washcloth, opening the pores and stimulating circulation.

While an occasional long bath or shower can be enjoyable, the bathroom is ideally used more efficiently for its obvious, intended purpose of purifying the body. Spending too much time immersed in water can actually weaken the kidneys and sexual organs, draining important minerals from the cells; prudent use of bath salts can minimize this concern.

Like beverages adulterated with preservatives, sugars, or high fructose or artificial sweeteners that damage the kidneys, body care products like shampoos, soaps, and toothpastes should also be comprised of natural substances. The bathroom (and the body) is no place for chemicals or synthetic colorings, dyes, or other contaminants—all the opposite of purification marketed to a cooperative public.

The kidneys and their complementary organ, the bladder, can be strengthened by quality vegetable protein found in beans and legumes, particularly those shaped like the organ itself. Regulating the proper amount of salt in the diet is the key to maintaining healthy kidney and bladder function, making certain not to go salt-free nor to use salt excessively. In fact, salt is the most important element in our diets, and for most of the world's great chefs, their most important seasoning.

Soft, absorbent bathmats, towels, and washcloths bring a natural balance to the tiling and porcelains found in most bathrooms and reflect the bladder function of holding liquids. Mirrors hanging over the sink should be kept as clean as possible to reflect our image without distortion; however, despite some people's obsession with hygiene, it is unwise to turn our bathrooms into sterile environments like operating rooms. Mild, natural cleansers, working fixtures, and proper air circulation do the job of ridding the bathroom of harmful waste without caustic chemicals.

Whites, off-whites, or lighter colors work best in an area like the bathroom where cleanliness is key; avoid using darker tones in bathroom areas, as doing so burdens the kidneys and moves us away from purification.

The Outer Landscape

The environment around our homes has changed as much as our interior spaces, but for many people, changes in nature beyond the daily weather forecast are less evident. Chemically treated lawns permeate many suburban landscapes, slowly poisoning the soil and water from which we draw our sustenance. While golf courses multiply, butterflies, honeybees, and frogs disappear by the millions. Simply stated, the human species is threatened more by our behavior as it relates to our environment than by any political, social, or economic factor. We need to totally reassess our place in the natural world and make drastic changes.

Permaculture, the harmonious intersection of landscape and people to provide food, shelter, renewable energy resources, and other needs in a naturally enduring way, is the next logical step outside our homes. The conscious design of productive ecosystems brings with it resilience and extraordinary diversity that we need to survive. Natural foods, natural fibers, and natural healing ultimately require natural ecosystems, and they aren't going to just magically appear.

The Planet We Call Home

The time has come to go beyond organic and natural, past New Year's resolutions to lose weight or stop smoking. We have reached a point in history where we have to pick up the tab, demanding that each household take stock of its impact on and place in the biosphere, from the microcosmic to the macrocosmic. Disciplines like permaculture begin with the new paradigm of the twenty-first century: designing our homes, villages, and communities with a profound respect for Mother Nature rather than an ignorant attempt to rule over her is no longer an option. It is a global imperative.

Responsibility

Responsibility does not only lie with the leaders of our countries or with those who have been appointed or elected to do a particular job. It lies with each of us individually. Peace, for example, starts within each one of us. When we have inner peace, we can be at peace with those around us.

Tenzin Gyatso,
His Holiness the Fourteenth Dalai Lama

Practicing feng shui helps us remember that there is really only one of us here—one human species. Nation states will continue to argue about boundaries, and religious leaders may attempt to guide us toward reconciliation, but no being can escape the interdependent nature of existence, the responsibility of relating to all sentient beings on the planet with humility, respect, and equanimity.

The "water" in "feng" is the sacred expression of our human blood—no nation, religion, or ego dwells there. The "wind" in "shui" is not that which rustles the leaves in the trees but truly signifies our next breath—essential for life itself. Only when we bring order to our blood, our breath, and our inner world can we look outside of ourselves with an understanding of, and appreciation for, the insepaarable bonds we share in this blessed life, on this fragile planet we call home. As we do, the heart of healing in feng shui brings us a place to start anew: inner peace.

Bibliography

Feng Shui, Geomancy, Architecture, Design, Puzzles, and Patterns

Alexander, Christopher. *A Pattern Language*. New York: Oxford University Press, 1977.

————. *A Timeless Way of Building*. New York: Oxford University Press, 1979.

————. *The Nature of Order*. Redwood, CA: CES Publishing, 2004.

Chang, Amos Ih Tiao. *Tao of Architecture*. Princeton, NJ: Princeton University Press, 1956.

Davies, Paul. *The Cosmic Blueprint*. New York: Simon & Schuster, 1988.

Eitel, Ernest J. *Feng Shui: The Science of Sacred Landscape in Old China*. London: Synergetic Press, 1984.

Gallagher, Winifred. *The Power of Place: How Our Surroundings Shape Our Thoughts, Emotions, and Actions*. New York: Simon & Schuster, 1993.

Groves, Derham. *Feng Shui and Western Building Ceremonies*. Dumfriesshire, Scotland: Tynron Press, 1991.

Hale, Jonathan. *The Old Way of Seeing: How Architecture Lost Its Magic (and How it Got it Back)*. Boston: Houghton Mifflin, 1994.

Lam, Kam Chuen. *The Feng Shui Handbook: How to Create a Healthier Living and Working Environment*. London: Gaia Books, 1995.

Lawlor, Robert. *Sacred Geometry: Philosophy and Practice*. London: Thames & Hudson, 1975.

Legeza, Laszlo. *Tao Magic: The Secret Language of Diagrams and Calligraphy*. London: Thames & Hudson, 1987.

Lip, Evelyn. *Feng Shui: A Layman's Guide to Chinese Geomancy*. Union City, CA: Heian International, 1987.

Makinson, Randell L. *Greene & Greene: Architecture as a Fine Art*. Salt Lake City, Utah: Peregrine Smith Books, 1977.

Mann, A. T. *Sacred Architecture*. Shaftesbury, Dorset [England]; Rockport, MA: Element Books, 1993.

McDonough, William. *Cradle to Cradle: Remaking the Way We Make Things*. New York: North Point Press, 2002

Mitchell, John. *The Earth Spirit: Its Ways, Shrines and Mysteries*. New York: Thames and Hudson, 1989.

Morgan, Jim. *The Wonders of Magic Squares*. New York: Vintage, 1982.

O'Brien, Joanne. *The Elements of Feng Shui*. Rockport, MA: Element Books, 1991.

Olivastro, Dominic. *Ancient Puzzles*. New York: Bantam Books, 1993.

Pauli, Gunter. *The Blue Economy: 10 Years, 100 Innovations, 100 Million Jobs*. Taos, NM: Paradigm Publications, 2010

Pearson, David. *The Natural House Book*. New York: Simon & Schuster, 1989.

Pennick, Nigel. *The Ancient Science of Geomancy*. New York: Thames & Hudson, 1979.

_____. *Earth Harmony*. London: Rider Book/Century Paperback, 1987.

Purce, Jill. *The Mystic Spiral: Journey of the Soul*. New York: Thames & Hudson, 1990.

Rossbach, Sarah. *Feng Shui*. New York: Dutton, 1983.

_____. *Interior Design with Feng Shui*. New York: Dutton. 1987.

Schimmel, Annemarie. *The Mystery of Numbers*. New York: Oxford, 1993.

Sharp, Dennis. *Illustrated Encyclopedia of Architects and Architecture*. New York: Quarto, 1991.

Sinclair, Cameron. *Design Like You Give a Damn: Architectural Responses to Humanitarian Crises*. Los Angeles, CA: Metropolis Books, 2006

Skinner, Stephen. *The Living Earth Manual of Feng Shui*. London: Arkana, 1989.

Swartwout, Glen. *Electromagnetic Pollution Solutions*. Hilo, Hawaii: Aerai, 1991.

Velez, Simon. *Grow Your Own House: Simon Velez and Bamboo Architecture*. Weil am Rhein, Germany: Vitra Design Museum, 2000

Walters, Derek. *Feng Shui: The Chinese Art of Designing a Harmonious Environment*. New York: Simon & Schuster, 1988.

Wilson, E.O. *Consilience: The Unity of Knowledge*. London: Little, Brown and Company, 1998

Wong, Eva. *Feng-Shui: The Ancient Wisdom of Harmonious Living for Modern Times*. Boston: Shambhala, 1996)

I Ching, Astrology, Divination

Anthony, Carol K. *A Guide to the I Ching*. Stow, MA: Anthony, 1988.

————. *The Philosophy of the I Ching*. Stow, MA: Anthony, 1981.

Blofeld, John, trans. *I Ching (The Book of Change)*. New York: Dutton, 1968.

Chung-Yuan, Chang. *Creativity and Taoism: A Study of Chinese Philosophy, Art and Poetry*. New York: Harper & Row, 1970.

Cleary, Thomas. *The Essential Confucius*. New York: HarperCollins, 1993.

————. *The Taoist I Ching*. Boston: Shambhala, 1986.

Dukes, Shifu Terence. *Chinese Hand Analysis*. York Beach, ME: Samuel Weiser, 1994.

Hazel, Peter. *Ancient Chinese I Ching: Consulting the Coins*. Selangor Darul Eshan, Malaysia: Pelanduk Publications, 1990.

Hoefler, Angelika. *I Ching: New Systems, Methods & Revelations*. Wilmot, WI: Lotus, 1988.

Huang, Kerson and Rosemary Huang. *I Ching*. New York: Workman, 1985.

Kushi, Michio. *Nine Star Ki: Introducing Oriental Astrology*. Becket, MA: One Peaceful World, 1992.

Lau, Theodora. *The Handbook of Chinese Horoscopes*. New York: Harper & Row, 1980.

Lingerman, Hal A. *The Book of Numerology*. York Beach, ME: Samuel Weiser, 1994.

Lorusso, Julia, and Joel Glick. *Strategems: A Mineral Perspective*. Albuquerque, NM: Brotherhood of Life, 1985.

Mann, A. T. *The Round Art*. Cheltenham, Great Britain: Dragon's World, 1979.

Ou-i, Chih-hsu. *The Buddhist I Ching*. Translated by Thomas Cleary. Boston and London: Shambhala, 1987.

Martin, William, Hank Tusinski, and Chungliang Al Huang. *The Sage's Tao Te Ching: Ancient Advice for the Second Half of Life*. New York: Marlowe & Company, 2000.

Palmer, Marrin, Kwok Man Ho, and Joanne O'Brien. *The Fortune Teller's I Ching*. New York: Ballantine Books, 1986.

Palmer, Martin. *Tung Shu: The Ancient Chinese Almanac*. London: Rider, 1986.

Post, James Nathan. *64 Keys: An Introductory Guide to the I Ching*. Cottonwood, AZ: Cottonwood, 1978.

Shchutskii, Iulian K. *Researches on the I Ching*. London: Routledge & Kegan Paul, 1980.

Sandifer, Jon. *Feng Shui Astrology*. New York: Ballantine Books, 1997.

_____. *Feng Shui Journey*. London: Judy Platkus, 1999.

Sherrill, W. A., and W. K. Chu. *An Anthology of I Ching*. London, Boston: Routledge & Kegan Paul, 1977.

_____. *Astrology of I Ching*. New York: Samuel Weiser, 1976.

Shimano, Jimmei. *Oriental Fortune Telling*. Rutland, VT: Tuttle, 1956.

Sorrell, Roderic, and Amy Max Sorrell. *The I Ching Made Easy*. San Francisco: HarperSanFrancisco, 1994.

Thompson, Gerry Maguire. *Feng Shui Astrology for Lovers: How to Improve Love and Relationships*. London: Thorsons, 1998.

Waley, Arthur. *Three Ways of Thought in Ancient China*. Stanford, CA: Stanford University Press, 1956.

Whincup, Greg. *Rediscovering the I Ching*. Garden City, NY: Doubleday, 1987.

Wilhelm, Hellmut. *Change: Eight Lectures on the I Ching*. New York: Pantheon Books, 1960.

Wilhelm, R. *I Ching or Book of Changes*. Translated by C. F. Baynes. Princeton, NJ: Princeton University Press, 1950.

Wing, R. L. *The Illustrated I Ching*. Garden City, NY: Dolphin Books/Doubleday, 1982.

Yoshikawa, Takashi. *The Ki*. New York: St. Martin's Press, 1986.

Yu-Lan, Fung. *A Short History of Chinese Philosophy*. New York: Macmillan, 1950.

Macrobiotics and Healing

Aihara, Herman. *Basic Macrobiotics*. Tokyo: Japan Publications, 1985.

Bates, W. H. *Better Eyesight Without Glasses*. New York: Holt, Rinehart & Winston, 1920.

Brown, Simon. *Macrobiotics for Life: A Practical Guide to Healing for Body, Mind and Heart*. Berkeley, CA: North Atlantic Books, 2009.

Colbin, Annmarie. *Food and Healing*. New York: Ballantine Books, 1986.

Dossey, Larry. *Healing Words: The Power of Prayer and the Practice of Medicine.* San Francisco: HarperSanFrancisco, 1993.

Emoto, Masaru. *The Hidden Messages in Water.* Translated by David A. Thayne. Hillsboro, OR: Beyond Words, 2004.

Ettlinger, Steve. *Twinkie, Deconstructed: My Journey to Discover How the Ingredients Found in Processed Foods are Grown, Mined (Yes, Mined), and Manipulated Into What America Eats.* New York: Hudson Street Press, 2008.

Galland, Leo. *The Four Pillars of Healing: How the New Integrated Medicine—the Best of Conventional and Alternative Approaches—Can Cure You.* New York: Random House, 1997.

Heidenry, Carolyn. *An Introduction to Macrobiotics.* Wayne, NJ: Avery, 1987.

_____. *Making the Transition to a Macrobiotic Diet.* Wayne, NJ: Avery, 1984.

Kushi, Michio. *Book of Do In: Exercises for Physical and Spiritual Development.* Tokyo: Japan Publications, 1979.

_____. *The Book of Macrobiotics.* Tokyo: Japan Publications, 1987.

Kushi, Michio and Alex Jack. *The Macrobiotic Path to Total Health: A Complete Guide to Preventing and Relieving More Than 200 Chronic Conditions and Disorders Naturally.* New York: Ballantine Books, 2003.

Lemer, Patricia S. *Envisioning a Bright Future: Interventions that Work for Children and Adults with Autism Spectrum Disorders.* Santa Ana, CA: Optometric Extension Program Foundation, 2008.

Lewis, Dennis. *The Tao of Natural Breathing: For Health, Well-Being and Inner Growth.* San Francisco: Mountain Wind Publishing, 1997.

Nishimura, Mayumi. *Mayumi's Kitchen: Macrobiotic Cooking for Body and Soul.* Tokyo: Kodansha International, 2010.

Northrup, Christiane. *Women's Bodies, Women's Wisdom.* New York: Bantam Books, 1994.

Ohsawa, Georges. *Cancer and the Philosophy of the Far East.* Oroville, CA: Georges Ohsawa Macrobiotic Foundation, 1981.

_____. *Essential Ohsawa.* Garden City Park, NY: Avery, 1994.

_____. *Philosophy of Oriental Medicine: Key to Your Personal Judging Ability.* Oroville, CA: Georges Ohsawa Macrobiotic Foundation, 1991.

Ornish, Dean. *Program for Reversing Heart Disease.* New York: Random House, 1990.

Porter, Jessica. *The Hip Chick's Guide to Macrobiotics: A Philosophy for Achieving a Radiant Mind and a Fabulous Body.* New York: Avery, 2004.

Sandifer, Jon. *Macrobiotics for Beginners: How to Achieve Health and Vitality the Oriental Way.* London: Piatkus Books, 2000.

Schumacher, E.F. *Small Is Beautiful.* New York: Harper Perennial, 1973.

Silverstone, Alicia and Neal Barnard. *The Kind Diet: A Simple Diet to Feeling Great, Losing Weight, and Saving the Planet.* Emmaus, PA: Rodale Books, 2009.

Tara, William. *Natural Body, Natural Mind: Health, Ecology and the Human Spirit.* Bloomington, IN: Xlibris Corporation, 2008.

Turner, Kristina. *The Self-Healing Cookbook.* Vashon Island, WA: Earthtones, 1987.

Verona, Verne. *Macrobiotics for Dummies.* Hoboken, NJ: Wiley Publishing, 2009.

Veith, Ilza. *The Yellow Emperor's Classic of Internal Medicine.* Berkeley: University of California Press, 1972.

Waxman, Denny. *The Great Life Diet: A Practical Guide to Health, Happiness and Personal Fulfillment.* New York: Pegasus Books, 2009.

Waxman, Melanie Brown. *Eat Me Now! Healthy Macrobiotic for Students and Busy People.* PublishAmerica, 2008.

Willmont, Dennis. *Fat Chance: Surviving the Cholesterol Controversy and Beyond.* Marshfield, MA: Willmountain, 2005.

Inspiration, Consciousness

Anthony, Carol K. Love. *An Inner Connection, Based on Principles Drawn from the I Ching.* Stow, MA: Anthony, 2002.

Boorstin, Daniel J. *The Discoverers.* New York: Random House, 1983.

Capra, Fritjof. *The Tao of Physics.* Boulder, CO: Shambhala, 1975.

Castaneda, Carlos. *The Art of Dreaming.* New York: Harper Collins, 1993.

_____. *A Separate Reality.* New York: Simon & Schuster, 1972.

Chen, Kaiguo and Zheng Shunchao. *Opening the Dragon Gate: The Making of a Modern Taoist Wizard.* Translated by Thomas Cleary. Boston: Tuttle Publishing, 1996.

Gladwell, Malcolm. *Blink: The Power of Thinking Without Thinking.* New York: Bay Back Books, 2007.

_____. *The Tipping Point: How Little Things Can Make a Big Difference*. Boston: Little, Brown, 2000.

_____. *Outliers: The Story of Success*. New York: Little, Brown, 2008.

Hayward, Jeremy W. *Perceiving Ordinary Magic*. Boston: Shambhala, 1984.

Jahn, Robert G., and Brenda J. Dunne. *Margins of Reality: The Role of Consciousness in the Physical World*. San Diego: Harcourt, Brace, Jovanovich, 1987.

Kabat-Zinn, Jon. *Wherever You Go, There You Are: Mindfulness Meditation in Everyday Life*. New York: Hyperion, 1994.

Lecomte du Noüy, Pierre. *Human Destiny*. New York: Longmans, Green, 1947.

Levine, Stephen and Ondrea. *Embracing the Beloved: Relationship as a Path of Awakening*. New York: Doubleday, 1995.

Marlow, Jennie. *Personal Magic: Creating Life, Love, and Work That Resonate with Your Soul*. iUniverse, 2003.

Millman, Dan J. *Way of the Peaceful Warrior: A Book that Changes Lives*. Tiburon, CA: H. J. Kramer, 1980.

Moyne, John and Coleman Barks. *Open Secret: Versions of Rumi*. Putney, VT: Threshold Books, 1984.

Nhat Hanh, Thich. *Being Peace*. Berkeley, CA: Parallax Press, 1987.

Ohsawa, Georges. *The Essential Ohsawa: From Food to Health, Happiness to Freedom*. Garden City Park, NY: Avery, 1994.

Rinpoche, Sogyal. *The Tibetan Book of Living and Dying*. San Francisco: HarperSanFrancisco, 1992.

Rumi, Jelaluddin. *Like This*. Athens, GA: Maypop, 1990.

_____. *The Ruins of the Heart*. Putney, VT: Threshold Books, 1981.

_____. *The Essential Rumi*. Translated by Coleman Barks. San Francisco: HarperSanFrancisco, 1995.

Sachs, Robert. *The Wisdom of the Buddhist Masters: Common and Uncommon Sense*. London: Watkins Publishing, 2008.

Sagan, Carl. *The Dragons of Eden*. New York: Ballantine, 1977.

Salzburg, Sharon. *Faith: Trusting Your Own Deepest Experience*. New York: Riverhead, 2002.

Senge, Peter M. *The Fifth Discipline*. New York: Doubleday, 1990.

Shapiro, Ed and Deb Shapiro. *Be the Change: How Meditation Can Transform You and the World*. New York: Sterling, 2009.

Trungpa, Chogyam. *Shambhala: The Sacred Path of the Warrior.* Boston: Shambhala, 1988.

Tsu, Lao. *Tao Te Ching.* New York: Vintage Books, 1972.

Wellwood, John. *Journey of the Heart: The Path of Conscious Love.* New York: Harper Paperbacks, 1996.

Index

About the Author

WILLIAM SPEAR is an internationally recognized educator, consultant, author, and lecturer on *feng shui*, the *I Ching*, integrative medicine, end-of-life care, and personal transformation. His clarity and ability to synthesize complex and diverse material is inspiring, insightful, and empowering.

In her introduction to William Spear's lecture at the Smithsonian in March 1997, Jan Stuart, Curator of the Smithsonian's Sackler-Freer Gallery, said, "William Spear is the ultimate Western authority on this ancient Chinese practice. He has taken feng shui beyond the confines of China to look at the importance of this art/science/philosophy in a broad international context and has achieved more than a historical or culturally biased view of feng shui to make it something modern and vital that affects our lives today." Hugh Pearman, the Architectural Editor of *The Sunday Times* of London, described Mr. Spear as *"the* feng shui man in the West."

Spear has been a consultant for hundreds of design projects from private residences to corporate offices, health clinics, and urban planning efforts. Because of his grasp of traditional, modern, and integrative medical practices, Spear advises many healthcare providers in the fields of degenerative disease, integrative medicine, and end-of-life care. At a recent international symposium on healthcare design, his presentation on "Understanding Environments that Nourish Body, Mind, and Spirit at the End of Life" was attended by major architectural and design firms at the forefront of innovative, research-based design practices implementing changes in leading medical centers throughout North America. He lectures regularly at various institutions and currently serves on the faculty of the Graduate Institute, Connecticut, where he teaches courses in the masters degree programs in Conscious Evolution, Holistic Thinking, and Experiential Health and Healing.

Spear's nonprofit Fortunate Blessings Foundation is dedicated to education for the larger ecological and social health of the human and natural community. His teachings consistently heighten public awareness of environmental issues, promote compassionate service to neighbors, and help individuals and businesses take actions that support the sustainability and systems of the natural world. The foundation's work includes studies on the effect of the environment on health, the relationship between diet and disease, and the care and support of people at the end of life. He has worked closely with hundreds of people with cancer and AIDS; survivors of nuclear accidents—especially children—in Chelyabinsk, Ukraine; and with families affected by the wars in Bosnia-Herzegovina and Kosovo.

Internationally, Spear also conducts educational programs and projects that focus on trauma care for children and families. Mr. Spear serves as a member of The Special Advisory Board for Developmental Delay Resources, a nonprofit organization dedicated to meeting the needs of those working with children who have developmental delays in sensory motor, language, social, and emotional areas. He is a regular contributor to the Huffington Post on the subject of trauma and disaster relief. In immediate response to the December 2004 tsunami disaster in South East Asia and also the May 2006 earthquake in Central Java, Indonesia, Spear led Fortunate Blessings Foundation teams of mental health professionals to assist orphaned and traumatized children. In both countries, he met with local officials, policy makers, child protective services, community organizers, relief workers, and others to devise strategies for coping with post-traumatic stress disorder. While in Java, he wrote and distributed the booklet *Care for Caregivers: Helping Children Work Through Trauma.*

At the heart of Spear's work are seminars that he has conducted since 1987 in North America, Europe, Indonesia, Africa, and Australia. These courses draw on more than three decades of assisting people who face life-threatening illness, loss of a loved one, bankruptcy, extreme trauma, and other immensely challenging issues. His counsel benefits anyone who may be inhibited from fully experiencing life in the present; in this regard, Spear has guided many small businesses owners, families, and the upper-level management of large corporations throughout the world as they grow and prosper. His current focus brings successful social media entrepreneurs together with socially conscious philanthropies that serve the most impoverished constituencies.

Spear regularly lectures at numerous international conferences and has appeared on a broad range of media in the U.S. and Europe, including features on CNN, the BBC, VH1, and the CBS Morning Show. He has spoken at the United Nations, appeared before the U.S. Senate Committee on Health and Aging, and addressed the National Academy of Sciences in Leningrad. Spear consults privately with a wide range of individuals, families, businesses, NGOs, and government officials. He maintains a private practice in Litchfield, Connecticut; New York City; and London.

To contact the author for additional information, courses, lectures, and private consultation services, please write or telephone:

William Spear
24 Village Green Drive
Litchfield, CT 06759
(860) 567-2535
inquiries@williamspear.com
www.williamspear.com